Writing Your Bestseller

L. Perry Wilbur

Piccadilly Books, Ltd.
Colorado Springs, CO

This book is dedicated to John Wilbur, Jr.,
a great nephew, friend, and e-mail partner.
May the Force be with you, Laurie, Jack, and Cole.

Copyright © 2010, L. Perry Wilbur
All rights reserved. No part of this book may be reproduced in any form without permission in writing from the publisher.

Piccadilly Books, Ltd.
P.O. Box 25203
Colorado Springs, CO 80936, USA
info@piccadillybooks.com
www.piccadillybooks.com

Library of Congress Cataloging-in-Publication Data

Wilbur, L. Perry.
  Writing your bestseller / by L. Perry Wilbur.
     p. cm.
  Includes index.
  ISBN 978-0-941599-81-8
  1. Authorship. 2. Authorship--Vocational guidance. I. Title.
  PN147.W485 2010
  808'.02--dc22   2010022928

Printed in the USA

Table of Contents

1: You Can Write That Book...5
2: The Truth About Writing a Bestseller.....................16
3: The Wide World of Nonfiction....................................24
4: What It Takes to Write a Novel.................................31
5: To Outline or Not: That Is the Question................37
6: Chapters Make the Book..42
7: How to Test Your Book Before You Write It........47
8: Working with a Literary Agent.................................51
9: Getting Along with Editors..57
10: Research and Interviews Add Depth....................65
11: When It's Time to Start Writing.............................70
12: Mining Ideas for Bestsellers...................................76
13: What About Length?..83
14: How Many Drafts Does It Take?.............................87
15: Writing the How-To Book..91
16: Addicted to Romance..97
17: Writing a Religious-Inspirational........................104
18: Business and Professional Books........................109
19: Textbooks Can Work for You..................................116
20: Don't Forget Humor Books!....................................120
21: Mass-Market Paperback Originals......................124
22: Ghostwriting Has a New Name.............................129
23: Promotional Opportunities....................................133
24: The Truth About Self-Publishing.........................139
25: Questions and Answers...144
26: Some Parting Advice...151

1
You Can Write That Book

If they ask you, you can write a book. And maybe another, and one more after that, followed by still more. You've heard the old saying that inside every person there's at least one good book. Practically every day someone utters the well-worn cliché: "I could write a book about it." The book you now hold in your hands is meant to help you do just that – and to do it well. It's also meant to show you how to sell your book, receive an advance (up-front money for it), and maybe make your book a bestseller.

Many people talk about writing a book but never get around to starting it. Many people like to think or talk about writing. They say they'll do it when they can find the time. Sadly, the time never comes. This book will prove to you that you can finish your own book manuscript. It follows logically that if you can write a book, you may also write a bestseller, sooner or later. The first book you write may be a dud, a fair-to-strong seller, or a blockbuster. You'll never know until you try.

The mere fact that you haven't written before could mean that you would bring a degree of freshness to the subject of your book. If you've already tried your hand at short stories, feature writing, a play, or perhaps the beginning of a novel, so much the better. Any writing experience you've had just means you're that much closer to a published book.

Writing a book is a challenge, whether it becomes a bestseller or not. Just completing a manuscript will give you an exciting sense of achievement. There's nothing quite like it.

Consider this. Bestselling author Harold Robbins usually had no idea what his books were going to be about when he began page one. The first page of a new book was always a challenge to him. He simply wrote the first sentence and took off from there.

Anne Wallach wrote her first novel, *Woman's Work*, in fourteen months, working on weekends only. The lead character in the novel is a dynamic woman in her late thirties who works for an advertising agency. Not given the salary, prestige, and privilege of the males in the agency, this woman struggles for recognition and love. New American Library, a mass market paperback publisher, took Anne's book for an incredible 850,000 dollars (at lot at that time or now). Mind you, this was her first novel. While such a large sum is rare for a first novel, it can and does happen. The book publishing business is full of surprises, and this is part of its allure and fascination.

Don't let the odds against you writing a bestseller – or just completing a book – bother you. If Columbus had worried too much about overwhelming odds, he might never have found the New World.

If you have an adventurous spirit, this book is for you. Writing a book, nonfiction or a novel, is a marvelous adventure. It's like having a child of your own and watching it grow. If the idea of bringing something new into the world appeals to you, you'll gain real satisfaction from writing. There will probably be other books written on subjects similar to yours, but none of them will be quite like the book *you* write. Why? Simply because there's no one else quite like you in the world.

Brand-name authors command much bigger bucks in the industry. Yet keep in mind that every well-known author was once a newcomer just starting out in the business. Big books like *Lake Wobegon Days, Texas, The One Minute Manager, Ladies of the Club*, and others quickly prove themselves in hardcover. So the major paperback publishers go after them, often bidding staggering sums of money in auctions to acquire the paperback rights.

The Prestige of a Bestseller

The money and prestige of a bestselling book is certainly worth shooting for in the business. While the percentage of big money authors may be a small one, those pulling in the big deals are smiling all the way to the bank and quickly launching their next books. When the national popularity of jogging was sweeping across the land, *The Complete Book of Running* was published. The author was a daily jogger himself, so he was able to do a first-rate book. He thought his book might sell perhaps thirty thousand copies. It did far better than that and earned Jim Fixx a tidy one million dollars in royalties in only 15 months.

Author Phyllis Dorothy James (P.D. James) worked on a book, *Innocent Blood*, early each morning before going to her daily job. She spent the evenings rewriting and polishing the manuscript, which is the way she has worked for many years. The money she earned from *Innocent Blood* was more than she made in 10 years as a senior administrator with the British government.

Erle Stanley Gardner, creator of the Perry Mason books, usually had seven or eight new book projects under way at all times. Naturally, he had a staff of secretaries and typists to help him maintain this kind of production.

Other strong-selling books have covered a variety of subjects, including *Growing Up Catholic, Bright Lights – Big City, Jaws, Gone with the Wind, Death of a President, Embraced by the Light*, and more.

Look over any list of bestsellers, and you'll notice that the books have a strong attraction for large numbers of readers. *The Joy of Cooking* is just one example. There must be many millions of people interested in the art of cooking, judging from the huge sales figures that get chalked up by various books on this subject. A book on cooking is timeless. It can be of equal value years from now.

Look at Your Future as a Book Writer

Let's say that you manage to write and sell at least one new book each year for the next five years. As an example, assume that four of your five published books sell just fairly well. Then say you get lucky and one book takes off, selling 100,000 copies. Depending on whether your books are hardcover or paperbacks (you may have some of each), you could easily earn 100,000 to 150,000 dollars from all five. This is an estimate of course and assumes some of the books do well in the marketplace.

If several of your books continued to sell in the coming years, you could make even more. You might not do this well.

Nobody really knows for certain what any one book will earn until after it's published and some indication of sales show on the accounts. This is another reason the publishing business is so interesting. There are frequent surprises.

The point of this example is to show you that you might have a wonderful future as a book writer. Once you develop your interest and ability to write, you might be able to finish two good books a year. It depends on you and the amount of time and effort involved in each book. Some writers spend three years or longer on a single work, but these are often long or very specialized books. If you write your books on a part-time basis (mornings, evenings, and on weekends), it will also take longer than it does for a full-time writer to finish one or more new ones.

It's true that most authors will never make it into the superstar leagues, but the fact remains that the potential is always there. A lot of money can be made, assuming a book gets some good breaks and that you're lucky. Look at a classic example, such as Peter Benchley's novel *Jaws*. The movie based on the novel broke box office records in its first weekend, exceeding seven million dollars in sales. The franchise has made several hundred million dollars since – and all this from a single book!

Before the first copy of *Coma* (another classic example) was published, the paperback and movie rights to the book had made Robin Cook a millionaire. He had done an earlier, fairly successful book titled *The Year of the Intern*. Cook was a surgeon when he did the book and a professor of medicine in Boston. His story shows that an author's first book may not do all that well but can lead to a highly successful second or third book.

Some authors don't attain substantial success with their writing until their tenth or fifteenth effort. If you're a real author, you'll want to keep creating more books. In my own case, after some 30 published books, I still feel the same as I did with my very first one. I see my books as my children, and I want to see them do well in the world. In a real sense, an author's first book is like giving birth. You never get over the pride of that first creation. No matter how many other books may follow, there's always a special place in your heart for your number one title – your baby.

Books Build Your Income Several Ways

There are several ways you can build a second income from the books you write and place with publishers. Advances and royalties add to your yearly take as an author. There are also subsidiary rights sales to magazines or newspapers, book club sales, and foreign rights monies. All of it together can add up to a good deal should your book carve a place for itself in a marketplace in which upwards of 65 thousand new books are published every year.

An advance is not a handout from a book publisher to an author; it's your own money you receive on the future earnings, the royalties, of your book. An advance means just that – an advance against the royalties to be earned by your book. When your book is published and selling in the stores, you won't get any more money until your book has earned back the amount of the advance. So the publisher gets back the money advanced to an author if and when the book starts to sell. Many books never earn back their advances. A number of others just break even. What every author shoots for, and publishers too, are books that will earn back their advances and then go on to earn a healthy profit.

The advance you receive from a publisher, after signing a contract, can help you financially while you complete your book. Many small publishers do not offer advances, but most of the major companies work this way. I've received a fair to good advance for each of the thirty-one published books I've written. For reprint deals (when a book is re-issued in an updated edition), an author can usually get the entire advance up front, rather than half on signing and the rest on delivery of an accepted, completed manuscript.

Once the book is published and selling, you will also receive royalty reports twice a year. For as long as your book sells, you receive royalties. They are sent to you in the spring and fall (usually), along with a statement of the number of copies sold, and any subsidiary rights sales such as serial rights, book club sales, or condensations in magazines and newspapers.

It's clear that the more books you write and place with publishers, the more royalties you will earn each year. You might, for example, only write and sell three or four books over a period of 10 years. If one or two of them, however, should become bestsellers, or even mini-bestsellers, your financial return could be substantial. You might also manage to write and sell one or two books a year for five or ten years in a row. As each new one starts to earn its way and earn royalties, your total income should naturally rise.

Some of the books you place with publishers may prove to be disappointing in sales. This is simply a fact of life in the business. Bad timing, the wrong cover, poor distribution, weak promotion, and other factors can hurt any new book being published. This is all the more reason to write and sell more books; it increases your chances of having some books that break through the odds and succeed in the marketplace. A famous mystery book author once made this interesting remark: "It's not any single title of my books that does real well but the combined total of all of my 20 books. That grand total brings me a very handsome income year after year."

This combined income from a number of published books was probably what drove Erle Stanley Gardner to keep multiple new Perry Mason book projects under way at all times. The total income from all his books was no doubt enormous, since more than 300 million of the Perry Mason books have sold worldwide.

The late author Isaac Asimov wrote and sold well over two hundred books in a period of about thirty years. The grand total, before his death, may be close to three hundred. Asimov's total number of books was constantly increasing because he could turn out a new manuscript so quickly. He typed ninety words a minute and did little rewriting. He didn't have to push himself at all and enjoyed his work.

On the other side of the picture, don't be discouraged if you happen to be a slow writer. The late Helen Hooven Santmyer spent a whopping 50 years writing her 1,344-page novel about life in small town Ohio. Her book, *And Ladies of the Club*, uses a women's literary club to chronicle life in a small town, covering the period between 1868 and 1932. Helen wrote this massive manuscript entirely in longhand in a bookkeeper's ledger. She was 88 years old and living in a nursing home when she finished it and became a literary sensation. The Book-of-the-Month Club made her book a main selection. It was featured in many leading publications, highlighted on all the major television talk and news shows, and became the most talked about literary property in decades. Being a slow writer should not keep you from getting one or more books written.

The happy news is that Helen Santmyer lived to see her book become a huge national success. When asked what advice she might give to other writers, she answered, "Believe in what you are writing…and finish it." She should be an inspiring example to all writers of the value and importance of not giving up. She persisted for an amazing *50 years* and only then saw her novel sweep the country.

Reasonable Proof There's a Book in You

Why am I so sure there's a book (at least one) in you waiting to be written? Because I know there are one or more subjects that interest you a great deal. You may even be an authority on some subjects. Such subjects are natural for a book.

If you've worked and lived long enough, you're bound to have accumulated ideas and opinions on anything from the art of living to farming to rocket science. Many readers would profit from a book by you on topics you know well.

You may know a lot about a certain type of business, the health field, cooking, nature, or any one of a hundred other subjects. Your own knowledge and information, along with the research you would do on the subject, could result in a helpful and interesting book.

Preview of the Pages to Follow

You'll learn in this book whether you should write a nonfiction book, a novel, or both. Chapter four will show you that ideas for new books are floating around every day. Just one big idea can get you started. You'll discover how to get power into your book chapters and keep the reader with you all the way to the last page.

Above all, you will learn what goes into a bestseller and how to do everything possible to make your book arrive on that coveted honor roll known as the bestseller list. All authors – the ones worth their salt, anyway – wonder if that may be their destiny.

Another section in the book will show you the way to sell your book to a publisher or editor. This alone can do a great deal to launch your career as a money-making book author. You want to sell your book and see it in print so it will have a chance on the national market, and perhaps even the world marketplace. This chapter tells you everything you must do to achieve this end.

Judging by all the books you see in the stores, the future of book publishing still looks bright regardless of good or bad economic periods. I will always remember what bestselling author Isaac Asimov said: "In good times or bad…people will always continue to buy books." Most publishers are optimistic about the coming years. While it's true that only a small percentage of new books published each year will become bestsellers, or blockbusters, there's always the chance that one of them will be yours.

Writing a book is as good a way as any to earn extra money today, and it may even be a bestseller if luck and the gods smile on you and your book gets some good breaks. It's a fairer and more interesting pursuit than most. The majority of those who write books are happy people who would not change their lifestyles for anything. George Sand, the French novelist who turned out a number of bestsellers in her day, said it well: "Books, ideas, and music; that's what life is all about." Most writers are not happy unless they're working on new projects. The more writing they do, the more they want to do.

I hope this book will influence you to decide now to become an author of books, even if you can devote only a few hours a day or week to it, or even just a bit of free time on weekends. That's enough time to get many books written and published over a period of months and years.

Who knows? One or more of your books might turn into big or mini-bestsellers. It could happen. This book will definitely increase the chances of it happening to you. Above all, this book will hopefully inspire you to go as far as your God-given talents allow in one of the greatest industries on our spinning planet, which is 21st century book publishing. Welcome aboard.

2
The Truth about Writing a Bestseller

     I now want you to banish from your mind the idea that one must be a genius to write a bestseller. It simply isn't true. The following realities should encourage you. Get them clear in your mind:

- A bestseller can be written on the first try, but the odds are against it. Peter Benchley did it with *Jaws*, and Clive Cussler with *Raise the Titanic*. *The Thorn Birds* was also a first novel.
- Publishers are definitely looking for authors, experienced and new ones, to write the bestsellers of tomorrow. You could be one of them. Some 65,000 new books arrive each year, and that means there are lots of authors to write them.
- A bestseller can cover any one of a variety of subjects.
- Many bestsellers have been written by authors 40 years old or more. Bestsellers are also written by authors in their early 20s up through the golden years.
- Bestsellers are written in the homes of authors, in hotels, motel rooms, in a cabin by the sea, on the beach, in formal

office settings, in bedrooms with just the mattress for a desk, or wherever.
- Imaginative publicity and promotion are what often turn a book into a bestseller.
- Some determined authors have "built" their books into big bestsellers by hitting the road and bookstores across the nation, while also doing radio and television interviews along the way. Author Sarah Palin's *Going Rogue* was already a huge bestseller, but she decided to continue promoting it by visiting major cities and signing copies of her book in key bookstores across America.

A Basic Truth About Bestsellers

A study of authors and novelists reveals that many of them, including the bestselling names, have to do a lot of writing before they get that big book. Not always, but this is usually the case. A good example is Barbara Taylor Bradford. During an interval of six years, she started four novels but discarded them all after a few hundred pages. She asked herself what she really wanted to write most and decided that it was a book about a girl in Yorkshire, England who builds a huge business empire. Barbara Taylor Bradford also wrote a number of nonfiction books, mostly on interior design. In her view, "A story is only interesting if it's about people. Their tragedies, their dramas, their joys." Her book about the Yorkshire girl evolved into *A Woman of Substance*, a very successful novel.

Once they have had their first novels published, numerous authors of fiction reveal that they wrote and experimented on one or more previous novels. In other words, few are lucky enough to sell the first fictional work they try. A period of time seems to be required during which a new author learns the craft. Many in publishing refer to it as "paying your dues." Relatively few authors slip through the publishing gates without paying their dues.

Still another common element of many bestsellers is the fact that the books took from one to three or more years to write. They were not dashed off in six months. Judy Blume spent almost three years on one of her books, which was a collection of letters from her readers titled *Letters to Judy: What Your Kids Wish They Could Tell You.*

To quote Barbara Taylor Bradford again, "A novel is a monumental lie that has to have the absolute ring of truth if it is to succeed."To achieve that vital ring of truth takes time. For most authors, it can't be run off in a few months. Again and again, we keep coming back to what has already been mentioned in this book – the statement and view of legendary author F. Scott Fitzgerald: "Writing a novel takes time." It seems too simple, too basic, a statement, but there's a lot of truth in it. You would be surprised how many would-be authors think they can turn out a book in a week or so. Some have done it, but their books were not exactly good reads.

Look at it this way. You have the chance to produce a bestseller on your very first try. If you fall short of your goal, you may well have at least a mini-bestseller. If not, then your first book – however many copies it sells – can pave the way for a bestseller on your second try, your third, and so on down the line. Once you've gotten your first book credits, you'll also find a warmer reception in publishing offices. Editors and publishers will be more interested in signing you up to write a manuscript. Most publishers prefer to deal with authors who have already proved they can turn out a creditable book. It's simply less risky for them that way.

Take a Look at These Current Bestsellers

At this time of writing, the following books are on the *New York Times* bestseller list. I urge you to watch these lists, for they can give you a great idea on what is selling and what kinds of books are in demand at that particular time. You can also compare what was selling five or ten years ago with the top sellers of today. Just keep in mind that such booklists, and titles on them, can become dated. I list the following ones to show you the variety of what readers out there are buying in large numbers:

Hardcover Fiction:
Under the Dome - Stephen King
U is for Undertow - Sue Grafton
The Lost Symbol - Dan Brown
The Help - Kathryn Stockett

Hardcover Nonfiction:
Going Rogue - Sarah Palin
Have a Little Faith - Mitch Albom

Paperback Fiction:
Push - Sapphire
The Shack - William Young
The Piano Teacher - Janice Lee
The Art of Racing in the Rain - Garth Stein

Producing a Bestseller

Keep in mind that the only way a book is ever written is through someone sitting down and writing it. So it stands to reason that the more you have thought about your book, nonfiction or novel, the better it will be. Ask the authors of bestselling novels how they do it, and many reply that "you have to live with your characters and get to know them so well that you're able to bring them to life on the printed page."

Authors also usually have someone in mind when they create their lead characters, and this may well help a book to be more believable. F. Scott Fitzgerald definitely must have had someone in mind when he created the character of Gatsby in *The Great Gatsby*.

I've given a lot of thought to the bestsellers of today, and I think that whether you're after a big novel or top notch nonfiction book, you must stay alert at all times for that *big idea* that's right for *you*. Bestselling author Clive Cussler says it this way: "You have to come up with a riveting concept for a novel." Cussler certainly did it when he asked himself an intriguing question: What if they raised the *Titanic*? This question and its answer led to his first bestselling book, *Raise the Titanic*. Since then Clive has produced a string of remarkable bestselling novels with Dirk Pitt as the fascinating hero in each of these spell-binding sea stories.

The same thing is true if nonfiction is your chief interest. You need a very strong idea, something fresh with wide appeal, a book that will *hook* readers – lots of them. There is already a glut of boring books on ho-hum subjects that don't offer enough interest for the majority of readers. Remember this: you are always competing with television, with the big movie screen, and other forms of entertainment and recreation.

Realize, too, that some authors are able to deliver the goods at a relatively young age. Other authors may not find their voices, or even start to write, until their late 30s, 40s, or beyond. The late Bruce Catton did not start his first novel until his 49th birthday. He eventually finished *Mr. Lincoln's Army* and later turned out the Pulitzer Prize-winning book, *A Stillness at Appomattox*. Bruce Catton proved that a person can turn to writing at a fairly late age and still become a highly successful author.

It should interest you that in the United States, the average age at which a novelist is first published is 40, and his or her novel is the *third* written. The magazine *Books in Canada* once published an article about a creative writing professor who had written a whopping 40 novels with only one published at the time to date! What I'm saying here is *fiction is usually tougher to sell,* in spite of the exceptions that come along from time to time.

Rod Serling (of "The Twilight Zone" fame) started writing fairly young, while still in military service. Known mainly as a television writer, Rod came, in time, to prefer books over writing for the tube.

The best dramatized scripts produced on the classic "Twilight Zone" were by far those of Rod Serling. He was light years ahead of the television writers of that era. He also wrote some superb scripts for the big screen. I had the distinct honor of corresponding with him, though I never had the pleasure of meeting him in person. He grew to hate the way so-called "script critics," having never written anything in their lives, would sit around a table in a Hollywood studio and pick his scripts apart, completely convinced they were experts.

Where Bestsellers Are Written

We touched on this earlier, but I believe more needs to be said here. Many newcomer authors believe they need a resort-like atmosphere in which to write and complete their books. The truth, once again, is that a bestseller can be written almost anywhere. Dr. Norman Vincent Peale penned a number of his successful books in a farmhouse in the country. Author James Michener did many of his bestsellers in a cabin. Incredible as it may seem, most of the research for *Nicholas and Alexandria* by Robert Massie was done in the New York Public Library and at Columbia University, yet many readers were convinced that the author spent a lot of time in Russia.

Some authors are able to write anywhere and everywhere. Others have to stick to one or a few basic locations. Until you learn where the words flow best for you, go ahead and experiment with different places.

Additional Truths About Writing a Bestseller

- Anyone who can write a simple sentence has the potential of turning out a bestseller. After all, every bestseller was written by adding one sentence after another.
- Word-of-mouth advertising has often helped turn a book into a bestseller. People buy the book and tell their friends, associates, neighbors, and relatives about it. The word

spreads, and sales keep climbing. This is the absolute best form of advertising.
- Views differ on how many sales mean a bestseller. Generally speaking, most consider a book that sells 40,000 copies or more to be a genuine bestseller.
- Whenever you read, hear about, or pick up a bestseller in the stores, think about the idea behind it. Why is it so popular? Is it a timely subject? Does the author have name recognition? How does the book deliver its front cover promise? Break down the reasons for its success, then try to get these factors into your own books.
- Faith in yourself and your book is very important. Without faith, nothing else matters. Faith will sustain you if your book should be rejected by a publisher. Just keep sending your manuscript to other publishers.
- Never forget that publisher, editors, and even agents are human and thus make mistakes. Numerous top-selling books were rejected many times. This includes the likes of *Auntie Mame*, which was turned down no less than 15 times by various publishers. Other rejected books were *The Day of the Jackal* (a big success that went to the screen as an four star film) and *Lust for Life*. *Jackal* was rejected by four major companies. I am still astounded by *Lust for Life*, the fascinating story of impressionist painter Vincent van Gogh. It was given a thumbs down by seventeen major publishers. It, too, became a blockbuster best film of that year, starring Kirk Douglas as Vincent van Gogh.
- You absolutely must take a great amount of trouble and time with your main character.
- Revisions are vital in getting a bestseller. Some successful manuscripts were rewritten three to eight times or more before selling. Rosemary Rogers wrote her romance novel 23 times

before sending *Sweet Savage Love* to Avon, where it was immediately accepted.
- The public's fancy can change very fast. You have just as good a chance to spot a developing trend as anyone else.
- By writing a book a year for a number of years, you can greatly improve your chances for one or more bestsellers.

Also, I urge you to send your book manuscript to a *specific* editor rather than send it in unsolicited, which is considered to be sending it in cold. I know you hear stories now and then about a manuscript being "plucked" off the top of the pile so to speak, as reports say the first *Harry Potter* book was, but your odds are much higher to first get a specific editor's interest and/or permission. Then send it in to that one person and pray.

Playing by the rules will increase your chances of getting your book accepted. That could mean you've passed one major hurdle on the way to a possible bestseller.

3
The Wide World of Nonfiction

You may well decide to cast your lot with books that are factual. The nonfiction book has great appeal for both new authors and veterans alike. Nonfiction offers you a wide world of writing choices, a veritable supermarket of possible subjects and ideas.

Although the novel makes periodic comebacks in popularity with readers, the nonfiction book remains the favorite type of reading for most of the book-buying public. Sales of books (fiction and nonfiction) will continue to rise through the coming years. There will be fluctuations, but on the whole the trend is upward. Nonfiction books still account for the largest chunk of the publishing pie

While there will always be people who buy novels for escape, most book buyers want to read what is true. Self-help books have been quite successful in recent years, along with religious-inspirational titles. Millions of readers everywhere want books that will help them in their daily lives.

Advantages of Nonfiction Over Fiction

Let's examine some of the natural advantages of writing a nonfiction book over a novel:

- A nonfiction book is usually easier to sell to a publisher.
- Chances are good that you already have some specific knowledge that could be used in a nonfiction book.
- A successful nonfiction book can sell one hundred thousand copies and higher. If a novel sells 35,000 to 40,000 copies, it's a bestseller. A great many novels fail to sell more than 5,000 copies.
- The odds of writing a nonfiction bestseller are more favorable than for a novel. The sales of first novels are usually very low.
- A wide variety of subjects is available to a nonfiction author.
- A nonfiction book may help many readers in some practical way by teaching, informing, persuading, entertaining, or inspiring them. Such books can change lives for the better.
- Nonfiction books often have a longer life in print than many novels.
- What is factual may be much more interesting to read than the product of a novelist's imagination. Truth is indeed stranger – and often more fascinating – than fiction.

A Nonfiction Book Is Easier to Sell

Generally speaking, it's easier to interest a publisher in a nonfiction book than in a novel. Why? A nonfiction book usually entails lower financial risk than a novel.

Publishers, as a rule, believe in sound business decisions. They're sometimes willing to gamble on novels or uncertain nonfiction, but most of them can't do it too often. They want to publish books that will earn back their investments and, hopefully, a substantial profit. Too many books on their list that lose money can mean trouble.

Another reason for sticking with the nonfiction book is the time-saving factor. Many publishers require anywhere from three chapters to all of the manuscript of a novel before a decision can be made. A nonfiction book, however, is often sold on the basis of an outline and one or two chapters. It's obviously far easier and more time-efficient to sell an outline and a portion of a book than to complete an entire manuscript on speculation.

In the time it would take to write a complete novel and sell it, you could close deals for several nonfiction books and probably even finish the writing on some of them. It can take years for a novel to make the rounds of publishers before finding a home. These realities are some of the main reasons that nonfiction authors do not switch to novels. Nonfiction books have treated them well in the long run. Even so, many nonfiction authors try their hand at an occasional novel.

Your Automatic Credentials for Nonfiction

One clear advantage of doing a work of nonfiction is the credentials you may already have going for you. Norman Vincent Peale had years of experience behind him as a minister when he sat down to write his bestselling inspirational book, *The Power of Positive Thinking*.

This is why there's truth in the belief that there's at least one book in everyone. You're bound to have some knowledge, work skills, personal insights, or specialized information that would be of help or interest to others. Search your mind. Clues may lie in hobbies, interests, civic work you do, or how you and your spouse saved your marriage. Other topics could include getting ahead financially, the right way to vacation in Europe or America, life in Australia today, your own system for success, camping in Canada, and thousands upon thousands of other possibilities.

I'm sure you get the idea. The world is filled with a limitless variety of people and no two of them are exactly alike. There are things you can do better than anyone else, and the same is true for your neighbors and other people you know.

Remember: it isn't a *must* that you be a recognized authority on a given subject. However, any formal credentials will certainly influence a publisher in reaching a favorable decision on your book project. You may have gained specialized information about a subject over the years, in special schools, through on-the-scene eyewitness experiences, or through your own natural talent and observations.

I got hooked on songwriting as a teenager and stuck with it for a number of years. I filled notebooks with things I learned about the music business. I made the rounds of music publishers in Nashville, New York, and Hollywood. I was on the scene for many country music festival-conventions in Nashville, and I met songwriters and artists there and at various meetings of the American Society of Composers, Authors, and Publishers (ASCAP). I learned a lot and, in time, had a number of my songs recorded and performed in nightclubs. Several songs won national awards. During the course of those years I wrote over a thousand songs.

When I thought later about writing a nonfiction book, a natural subject for me was a book on songwriting and the thriving music business. I sold this first book to the very first publisher I contacted. The book was published in both hardcover and paperback as *How to Write Songs That Sell*. It became a steady backlist seller and remained in print for almost 10 years.

Successful Nonfiction Books Sell Big

Aside from the blockbuster mass-market novels – often paperback reprints from earlier hardcover editions that sold well – novels don't often sell as well as nonfiction. Naturally, a proven name is a guarantee of a big-selling novel. Yet the average novel without a name behind it does not usually sell nearly as well as the average nonfiction book.

Many publishers are happy if some of their novels sell 6,000 copies. If a publisher can get its investment back – plus a profit – he's often pleased. This is especially true for most first novels.

There are occasional exceptions. Sometimes a novel will catch on, no matter who wrote it, even though it may be the author's first work.

Nonfiction Books Can Sell Better and Longer

James Herriot's books about animals can go on selling for years to come. These books have a timeless quality about them. The late Sam Levenson once wrote a book called *Everything But Money*. In its second year of publication, it sold from 2,000 to 4,000 copies a week. Within 15 months after publication, 310,000 copies had been sold. Sales kept growing and it continued to sell.

The Odds Are Better for Nonfiction

Unless you're convinced that you can come up with a mass-market novel, your chances of writing a bestseller are greater with a nonfiction book. One good example of a continuously selling book was *English the Easy Way*. Norman Schachter, the author, won a Gold Book Award for the first million copies sold. The book went on selling for years.

Look at it this way. As an author, you're more likely to earn a lot of money on a book that can keep selling for years than you would on a title that stops selling in several months. Since you're investing your time and effort in writing new books, why not strive to produce titles that will sell for years to come? It makes good sense.

You'll realize sooner or later that you have many interesting nonfiction subjects to write about. Knowing this keeps many authors encouraged and enthusiastic about their work. If one book doesn't advance toward the bestseller list, another one may do so. In other words, the nonfiction book just seems to offer more potential. On the other hand, how many great novel ideas could you come up with as the years go by? There are a number of authors who write novels in-between nonfiction books. Nonfiction is their bread and butter, and once they discover it they think seriously before switching to a novel. Such writers, however, will try a novel on occasion, as a change of pace from factual books, and also to play an occasional long shot. This method combines both types of writing. The only problem is that many authors cannot do both kinds of books; they have to concentrate on one or the other. You should try to find out whether you can write both fiction and nonfiction, or if you need to focus on just one kind of book.

A Wide Variety of Subjects

Once again, I cannot stress too much how appealing the nonfiction book is because of its unlimited subject matter. The choice of things to write about is endless: how to quit smoking, patriotic books about America, books on divorce, the stock market, money-making, sex, raising the kids, the current economy picture, humor books, and on and on.

Every time you visit a good-sized bookstore, try walking through the entire store rather fast. As you do, glance over the variety of book categories and the kaleidoscope of subjects available to readers. Notice how many nonfiction titles await a buyer. If you browse in a couple of large bookstores a least once a week, you're almost certain to get a good idea of the panoramic array of current nonfiction titles for sale.

Here's the payoff. The many titles that catch your eye will get your mind into the book groove sooner or later. Make it a regular habit to browse in some bookstores every week. If you do, you will soon have new book ideas whispering in your ears and clicking in your mind. You'll naturally want to pick up the books that interest you. Glance at the jackets, read the copy on them, look over the contents pages, and perhaps read a few pages here and there. Such a routine, if done consistently, will help to keep you book oriented.

Actually, bookstore browsing can lead to the marvelous discovery that you're a potential author. Whether you're a beginner, a newcomer with little experience, a sometime published writer, an established professional, or just a person with general interest in the book field, it can be profitable for you in your own writing. Seeing all those fresh books for sale can increase your desire to write and determination to become a successful author.

After visiting bookstores regularly for some weeks or months – and of course buying new books that appeal to you – you should eventually feel a growing desire to write a book of your own, to bring your own printed baby into the world. Most authors are avid and enthusiastic readers. You should even, on occasion at least, feel tings of excitement wandering through bookstores. It's also fun to imagine your own books are on sale in the stores.

One way, in fact, to discover your own talents is to wonder what it would be like to visit a local bookstore and see one of your own books. If such a thought fills you with enthusiasm, maybe you should start writing that book. It might be the start of a wonderful career for you, or a fascinating sideline pursuit.

4
What It Takes to Write a Novel

Each time you write a book, you have a choice of doing either a nonfiction book or a novel. Let's take a look now at the possibilities of writing a novel. Actually, your decision to write either type of book is an important one. Some writers write both types of books. Others prefer to stick with just one type. The kind of book you read most often is a big clue for the type of book you should write.

What Is Needed to Write a Novel
- A good idea and the desire to develop it.
- The time and freedom to write.
- An intriguing character, preferably caught up in conflict.
- A title, theme, mood, or feeling.
- Concrete observations.
- Discipline.

Let's look at each of these views on what is needed to produce a novel all your own.

A Good Idea and the Desire to Develop It

There's no guarantee that if you get a good novel idea in your head you're going to actually develop it. Many people have probably thought of good ideas for novels but then never got around to finishing even the first page.

A good idea coupled with the desire to develop it can form a strong combination. If the desire to write is there and the idea keeps asking to be developed, this may be enough to get you started.

First, novelists can often come up with all sorts of reasons why they should not start work on a novel. The success of the venture depends on the author's determination. On a trip to Nashville for research and to do an article on the Grand Ole Opry, Garrison Keillor was intrigued by the format of the Opry show. On his return to St. Paul, he began to work Lake Wobegon bits into his radio show. Tom Clancy was fascinated by the idea for a novel about the defection of a Soviet submarine crew, and this gripping idea eventually became his enormously popular and bestselling novel, *The Hunt for Red October*. His book sold millions of copies in paperback and hundreds of thousands in hardcover.

The Time and Freedom to Write

Who knows how many people from all walks of life have said "If I only had the time and freedom to write, I'd turn out a hell of a novel." It's one thing to talk about writing a novel and something else to actually do it.

The time and freedom to write have made it possible for some people to complete their novels. George Sand (her pen name) left her home, husband, and children for the time and freedom to write in Paris. She cared little for her husband, but missed her children terribly. At first she arranged to spend six months of each year in Paris and the other six back at home. This freedom and time to write encouraged her to develop good work habits early. She had a goal of writing no less than 20 (some reports say 30) pages each night. She wouldn't retire for the night until she had finished her regular stint with paper and pen. It was one of the reasons for her success and helped make her an established author. Her amorous adventures, outspoken opinions, and daring (for that era) novels all combined to make George Sand the talk of Paris before she was 30.

An Intriguing Character

A character can be so vital that the writer eventually feels compelled to give him or her life on paper.

Imagine what it might be like to see and hear a Scarlett O'Hara, Oliver Twist, or Claudius in your mind, to "live with them" as their personalities take shape in your head. Many successful novelists do just that. Such an "incubation period" pays off. They live with their characters a long while before getting them into a book, and often write a stronger, more readable book than they otherwise would have.

When you write fiction you are speaking *with* character and action, not *about* character and action. It's wise to introduce your lead character in the very first paragraph of your novel, or as soon thereafter as possible. If you can, try as well to present the situation, or at least part of it, in the first paragraph. Situation involves the locale of the story as well as the relationships in which the characters find themselves. Every novel is a story of character, and characters in fiction can be developed by action, reaction, explanation, effect, and speech. The story of a novel moves forward through the use of dialogue.

A Title, Theme, Mood, or Feeling

Sources of novel ideas are numerous. Actually, your own life can yield good ideas. Something you read in a book, magazine, or newspaper can set the wheels in motion. Many authors keep a sharp eye out for those little one or two paragraph stories you see on the back pages of most newspapers. The seeds of some bestselling novels have been found there.

Sometimes all you need is the initial spark or idea association. A title might leap out at you from the printed page or come to you while you're walking the dog or taking a shower. A feeling you have on a rainy day, a sad, depressed, or happy mood, or even just a phrase may all suggest a possible novel.

Ray Bradbury's advice is quite helpful indeed. Often asked where he got his ideas, Ray's reply is memorable. "All of the good, weird stories I've written are based on things I've dredged out of my subconscious. That's the real stuff. Everything else is fake." As a young girl growing up in Atlanta, Margaret Mitchell heard many true stories about the Civil War. So it was natural that her novel idea was a story about the early south.

Discipline

One of the most useful tools for getting a novel (or any book) written is discipline. An author may lack the freedom and time to write, but still be able to finish several novels thanks to discipline. It's a very valuable commodity.

James Michener spent years of work on his fine novels like *Poland* and *Space*. He was well-known for the pains he took to present the history of the area (state or country) through which he wove his characters and story.

In Barbara Taylor Bradford's view, there's only one reason to write a novel: "That is because writing fiction is absolutely essential to one's well-being. In other words, it's the work that really counts, the sense of creation."

Ray Bradbury put it this way: "All you should worry about is whether you're doing it every day and whether you're having fun with it. If you're not having fun, find the reason. You may be doing something you should not be doing."

Novels are composed of scenes, and it takes discipline to get those scenes right and believable. When each scene ends, the reader should know something more and feel something more. Famous author F. Scott Fitzgerald said it in a special way: "To make the reader see is an author's main purpose." That requires the discipline to rewrite until you have it right. Fitzgerald also said this about the act of writing itself: "You must begin by making notes. You may have to make notes for years. Put an idea down when you think of it. You may never recapture it quite as vividly the second time." Emotion was part of the total mix for Fitzgerald. "Whether it's something that happened 20 years ago or only yesterday, I must start out with an emotion – one that's close to me and that I can understand."

Think of the discipline of Ernest Hemingway in his early writing years. For years he got pitifully small checks from little magazines. But he kept at it and eventually became a very successful author – one of the giants of modern literature.

Types of Novels to Write

If you believe that novel writing is for you, there's an interesting choice available to you. Whether you're a beginner or a veteran, looking over the various types of novels you might write can be helpful. Most of the main genres are included in the following list:
- Adventure novels
- Suspense and crime thrillers
- Romances
- Mysteries
- Science fiction novels
- Occult and supernatural novels
- Gothics
- Fantasy novels
- Horror novels

- Mainstream novels
- Historical novels
- Juvenile or young adult novels

The above isn't a complete list, but it includes several of the types of novels you might experiment with in the course of a career.

I want to emphasize here that the science fiction novel is very popular from time to time and can remain so for extended periods. The many films about space and similar series programs on television have sent the sales of this novel category soaring at various times.

Before ending this chapter, I want to highlight two very important abilities for success as a novelist. One is being a good storyteller, and by that I mean having a strong talent for telling interesting tales. The other is being able to write well, so that it comes alive on paper. I also mean by this the ability to use interesting sentence structure and to express yourself well in writing.

You may have a great story to tell, but it can't be shared if you can't get it on paper. Now here is the four-star point about both of these abilities. Both are vitally important for substantial success as a novelist. But in my opinion, being a good, effective story teller is more important. If you have a gripping story, there are editors who will help you get the material into shape.

So when and if you come up with a riveting tale, idea, and story for a novel, you're already halfway home. If you're weak in story and plot development, you can always improve over time. That's a major fascination about novel writing: there is always more to learn about writing them and making it all happen between the covers.

5
To Outline or Not: That Is the Question

❖ ❖ ❖

Whether you write one book or twenty, the idea of using an outline is worth some time and thought. In the case of nonfiction books, most authors find it helpful to make an outline first. For novels, many authors won't use an outline. Others will go to great pains to plan each chapter carefully before writing.

So the basic question of whether or not to use an outline usually depends upon the particular person involved and his or her own feelings and work habits. Let's look at some of the advantages and disadvantages of using an outline.

An Outline Is a Track to Run On

A sound reason for using an outline is the simple fact that it gives you a track to run on, a road map to follow.

It's often easy to outline an article in your mind. A book is a much longer piece of work. Books call for a basic plan, a well-organized blueprint that shows how you intend to complete the project.

People from all walks of life have remarked, on occasion, that they could write a book and that they were going to do it someday. Most of them are dreaming out loud. Some of them would actually be amazed at the books they could complete if they would take the time to learn how to do an outline.

An outline is like a series of signposts for an author. It lets the writer see, on paper, how a book will begin, develop, reach a climax (especially if a novel), and end. Outlines are like beacons; they light the way for an author when the going may be rough. They steer authors through dangerous waters and help to keep them off the rocks.

A Promising Outline Can Sell Your Book

One of the strongest reasons for doing an outline is because it can help to sell your book before you've written a word of it. This is especially true for nonfiction books.

Quite a few nonfiction authors have sold their books to editors based on just an outline and sample chapter. I've done it myself a number of times. Some of my previous books, on business and other subjects, were sold from outlines only. What this means is that if an outline you create and send to an editor shows enough promise for a finished book, you will know the happy feeling of receiving an offer for your book.

It's true that many editors will want to see more before reaching a decision – perhaps a chapter or two along with the outline. But never forget that a lot of authors sell their books with just a strong outline. It's being done every day. Just keep in mind that your outline must be a good one.

Outlines Grab Attention

A number of authors have been successful at grabbing an editor's attention with an outline. The author first sends a complete outline or a synopsis of the project. If the editor expresses interest, several sample chapters can be sent. So an outline can be used as a teaser, a means of testing an editor's interest.

You'll learn with experience that requirements vary with the editor and publisher. Some editors will make a decision based on an outline alone, particularly if you've already been published. Other editors need an outline and one or two chapters before reaching a final decision.

What Goes Into a Book Outline?

Novels
The best outline gives a clear idea of what happens in each chapter of the novel. This way the entire work can best be evaluated and considered. Some outlines also include the theme and plot, along with a description of the main characters, the conflict of the story, how the complications build to a crisis, resolve in the climax, and how the whole story is brought to an end.

Nonfiction Books
A basic statement regarding the purpose of the book can be helpful. Many outlines for this type of book include a table of contents with a description (a paragraph or section subtitles) of what each chapter will cover.

Outlines based on variations of the descriptions have of course been written and accepted, with or without the editor's request for some sample chapters.

Length of the Outline

As you've probably guessed, an outline for a book may run from one or two pages to twenty, thirty, or more. If the outline gets to be too long, it may defeat its purpose.

The length seems to depend on the particular author and the type of book involved. As a general rule, don't let your outlines run too long. Authors have been known to exhaust themselves on the outline when it's the book that deserves the bulk of their attention and effort. Don't wear yourself out on the outline so much that you have no energy left for the book itself.

Specific Lengths

Paperpack Originals (Novels)
Most run from 50,000 to 80,000 words. Certain adventure books and some romances may run 100,000 words and over. Saga type novels tend to run 500 pages and more.

Nonfiction Books
Most run from about 50,000 to 80,000 words. Juvenile and young adult books usually run about 40,000 to 50,000 words.

Special Note
At this time in the book marketplace, books in general are tending to run a bit shorter than in previous years. You should watch the trend and know when it changes back to longer books. Over several decades you will see the length of books alternating between long to shorter trends. Being aware of this can help you sell your new book.

Know the Book You Intend to Write

It helps to know something about your main characters when beginning a novel, along with knowledge of the setting. Some degree of planning for a novel is a must whether you put it into a specific outline or not.

You will need to experiment to see what works best for you. Using an outline for one book doesn't mean that you're stuck with one on all future books. Just go with what each project seems to require.

Remember that a promising outline for a nonfiction book can go a long way toward selling your project to an editor – before you write the first word of the manuscript. So unless novels are your forte, sound outlines for nonfiction books will probably mean more book sales for you in the long run.

Why Some Authors Dislike Outlines

Different authors give their reasons in various ways. In general, here are the reasons why some authors turn thumbs down on using an outline:
- Outlines can be restrictive.
- The minds of many authors go blank when they have to make an outline.
- Authors are often more stimulated by working from an opening sentence, setting, or character introduction.
- Some authors simply see little or no use for an outline.
- "Outlines are flat and cold" is the reason given by a number of authors.
- An outline may be a poor indicator of the final book. The completed book may turn out far better than the outline suggested. Yet editors may turn the project down if they don't like the outline.

Good luck whichever way you go. You're bound to find what works best for you through experience. Keep in mind that you can always tear up an outline, change it to please yourself, or do a brand new one. You may also focus on nonfiction books and never choose to do a novel. Some authors prefer to only write novels. I like doing both and discovered some years ago that writing fiction can relieve the nonfiction pace and help to keep you fresh.

To outline or not to outline? Let it be a new question to answer for each new book that will bear your name.

6
Chapters Make the Book

It may sound obvious, but try to keep one fact about writing books in mind at all times. Chapters make your book. This basic truth can help you finish any number of projects. Chapters are the framework of your book. You can sustain your enthusiasm by realizing that you draw ever nearer to a book's completion with every new chapter you finish.

Don't underestimate this truth. Many people who consider writing a book never do it. An important reason why they never do is that the thought of all the work involved scares them. It can be frightening to think of the work required for a book, regardless of the length.

So don't let your book project leer at you with the amount of work needed to become a reality. Seeing all that work in one massive dose can depress even the most prolific of authors.

Your salvation lies in chapters. By breaking the total project down, you're not overwhelmed by the sheer magnitude of it. You may not see how your book will end, or even see its middle part. Don't worry about it. Just concentrate on doing one chapter at a time.

Give your attention to the chapter at hand. When you're satisfied with it, move on to the next. Chapters have a marvelous way of adding up, just as pages do also. Focus on the bits and pieces of your project – the words, sentences, paragraphs, pages, and chapters. These will all work together to produce the beginning, middle, and end of your book.

Look at it this way. If you wrote just one page a day for the next year, you would have a book of 365 pages. Or you could do the same by writing two pages a day for six months. The work schedule you set and stick to is up to you.

Planning Chapters in Advance Pays Off

Some authors develop various ways to keep making progress on their books. One, for example, plans his next chapter whenever he finds himself bogged down with a current one. This way he doesn't lose valuable time.

A lot of writers work hard on the advance planning of chapters. Such work pays off when they are ready to begin the actual writing of the book. After you complete chapter one, you already have a script prepared for chapter two – and know where you're heading with the material. You can't get stuck because you always know where to go next. That's the result of advance planning. It keeps your progress moving forward smoothly and continually.

Advance planning of chapters can be another source of enthusiasm. You're eager to get into the next chapter because the plan for it is ready and waiting. The total effort results in increased confidence as your book comes to life.

Chapter Headings Stimulate Your Writing

While some novels don't have any chapter headings, most nonfiction books make use of them. Chapter headings can even increase the sales of your book. Watch how many browsers and customers in bookstores skim through books, glancing at the chapter headings. Many will decide to buy a particular book if the chapter headings offer promise of good reading.

What is more important is the fact that well-written chapter headings stimulate your writing all through your book. Some will interest you more than others, but all of them act as signals. They tell what each chapter is about and what the reader is likely to find there.

Vary the Length of Your Chapters

Never forget that all readers are human. Give them some variety in the length of your chapters. Don't follow a long chapter with too many others of the same length. Break up the pace now and then.

If properly placed in a book, short chapters provide relief and help the readers feel that they are making progress in finishing the book. No reader likes to feel that reading is a chore. In other words, make the reading journey as easy and clear as possible.

Readers often take a rest or refreshment break after finishing a chapter. If many of your chapters are too long, your readers may have to stop in the middle or end of a page in order to take their breaks. No author can ever be certain that those who buy a book will read it straight through at one sitting. It's nice to think that at least some people might do so. But more people enjoy variety in the books they read, and reading habits, along with comprehension levels, differ. So help the reader along with variety in your chapter length, style, and presentation.

Some Chapters Are Tougher Than Others

Any author knows from experience that some chapters are harder to write than others. It's par for the course. Whether you write one book or thirty, you'll soon discover this for yourself. Some chapters almost write themselves. The work seems to flow.

The material seems fresh and vibrant. The writer is enthusiastic and may even feel sad to reach the end of such chapters.

Not so with other chapters. Any author may get stuck at any point. If and when this happens to you, don't force it. If you get bogged down, try one of the following remedies:
- Take a break. Relax and think about something else for a while. You will come back refreshed and better able to solve the problem.
- Liquid refreshment may help. Have a soda, coffee, tea, or glass of fruit juice. Nothing stronger. Remember, you're writing. Liquor and writing don't mix well.
- Take a brisk walk for 30 minutes or so.
- Try reading the material out loud. This can help.
- If nothing seems to work, knock off work for a few hours or even until the next day.

Once they have their book outlines, some writers go through them and mark the chapters they feel will be most interesting or easiest to write, and those that will be the toughest. Then they can alternate between writing difficulties, first completing an easy or interesting chapter, then moving on to a tougher one. Some authors, of course, find every chapter hard to write, while the lucky ones enjoy working on every single part of their books.

Chapter One Sets the Theme of Your Book

I hope you already realize the importance of the first chapter. This is your grand opening. The spotlight is on your beginning sentences. The reader's attention is focused on your words.

In the case of novels, the first few paragraphs may well determine whether your book sells. Many a prospective book buyer will read the first page before making a decision to buy or not. Nonfiction book buyers may read half or more of the first chapter before deciding whether or not to buy. This is especially true if the opening chapter is fairly short.

If sent with an outline to an editor, your first chapter can mean the difference between the sale of your work or a rejection. No wonder most authors rewrite the first chapter of each of their books several times. They know it's that important.

Make Your Last Chapter as Good as the First

A sound rule for writing books that will sell is to do all in your power to make your last chapter just as strong as the opening one. Actually, this rule should apply to every chapter. Do your best on each one, and you'll never feel sorry later that you didn't give a particular chapter your best effort.

Remember, it's too late after your book is in print. Once published, that's it until a future edition, if any, is published. That may never happen. So do your best all the way through your book. Then you will know that the greatest possible effort went into writing an effective and worthwhile book.

Whether your book sells 5,000 copies or 100,000, you'll be proud in the knowledge that you gave your project your best. Who could ask for anything more?

7
How to Test Your Book Before You Write It

❖ ❖ ❖

Since most editors have no spare time, a strong case can be made for first sending a query letter regarding your idea. Editors appreciate this consideration and will be able to respond more quickly because of it.

The query letter has grown considerably in importance in recent years. Many editors of books and magazines say they much prefer a query first and deem it a requirement in dealing with them. The advantage of the e-mail query (or snail mail letter) is that it allows you to sell your book before it's even written. It hits the editor with your basic book idea, and if the editor likes the sound of it, he or she will probably want to see more.

A query also gives the editor an idea of your writing style, shows the range of your thoughts about the subject of the book, and provides hints as to whether your basic idea and choice of subject indicate a worthwhile project. A good query letter can convince an editor that you have what it takes to complete a book.

It makes sense to find out if an editor is receptive to your new book idea. Most publishers develop a certain kind of book list over the years. A cookbook, for example, or a title on investing, or any number of other subjects may be completely wrong for a given publisher.

The author saves time, and so does the editor, when you first send a query letter. You would be surprised how many would-be authors send off their manuscripts to publishers with no knowledge of what a particular company specializes in. Cookbooks should not be sent to a publisher who produces detective novels. Religious books sometimes arrive in the offices of a craft or gardening publisher. An author must fit the book to the right publisher.

A go-ahead response to a query letter is no guarantee of acceptance of your book once it's completed or enough of it to show is ready. A yes response does, however, often signal an editor's interest in your idea and possible desire to see an outline and a few sample chapters.

Hit Them With an Idea First

Let us assume that you have come up with a new and worthy book idea. You like it and believe it would sell. How do you present your idea to publishers? Here are some choices open to you:
- Describe your idea briefly in a letter consisting of anywhere from a few paragraphs to a full page.
- Give a clearer description in a two-page letter.
- Describe your idea in a letter to a dozen publishers and offer to follow up with an outline and sample chapter. This is the multiple submission method. Numerous authors report good results from using it. You can send multiple query letters and also multiple outlines and chapters to a dozen or more publishers.
- Hit the editor you write or phone (they don't usually like calls) with a working title. This can help keep the book idea better fixed in the editor's mind.

- Simply state that you want to write a book on a given subject and tell why you believe it might be right for that publisher. Do this for each company you contact.
- Ask the editor if there is current interest in new book projects. Name the categories that include your book ideas such as self-help, how-to, children's books, adventure novels, romances, or whatever. Most people in the industry think of romances, westerns, mysteries (and certain other types) as genre books.

Most editors discover through experience that good publishing ideas come from virtually anywhere. A taxi driver once made a remark to a Harper and Row (now Harper-Collins) editor, "I wish someone would write a book describing a thousand ways to amuse a child." Harper's policy at the time was to pay 100 dollars to anyone who suggested a book idea that they accepted. A bit later, Harper's published a book based on the driver's idea: *838 Ways to Amuse a Child*. The book did well and sold for many years.

Good Idea but the Wrong Publisher

A good way to handle this matching of a book idea with the right publisher is to request the latest catalogs from publishers. If you have access to the Internet you can view almost any publisher's catalog online. After studying them over, pick the companies you believe you will have a realistic chance of selling.

Remember that the titles listed in a catalog may not be what an editor currently wants. Maybe the publisher has decided to change its line of books. So ask the editor if the books listed in the catalog are a good indication of what is wanted.

A while back, I sent a major publisher a general nonfiction book project. The editor had given me his okay to send any new project I thought right. I got a nice reply a few weeks later. He called the outline and chapters I had sent "a model plan for a book." Unfortunately, his company did not publish books on that particular subject. Try to be certain that the subject of your book is one done by that company.

The Practical Way to Sell Your Book

Don't write a complete manuscript unless you have the time and are willing to gamble on a finished manuscript. Describe your book idea first to some editors to get their reactions. If they like your idea, they'll ask to see more. Then you can send an outline and a sample chapter or two. If you value time, and most people do, it makes sense to sell your book this way.

Why spend time and effort to do a complete manuscript unless you have a firm commitment from a publisher in the form of a contract and advance? Many professionals test ideas first and then go ahead with an outline and a few chapters.

Publishers vary on how much material they need to see from a novel. Some will decide on three chapters and a synopsis of the rest. Others prefer a complete manuscript. So, first find out what a specific publisher requires.

It's very nice to know that the manuscript you're working on has already been sold. You have signed a contract and hopefully received a good advance. Thus, there will be no doubts that the book will have a home. You know it's going to be published, unless you fail to do a good job on the rest of the book.

With time and some experience behind you, you will come to appreciate the wisdom of testing and selling a book project before writing the complete manuscript, or even part of one. That's the professional way to do it.

8
Working With a Literary Agent

Frankly, it puzzles me why so many people are often amazed when an author sells a book without an agent. It happens every day. Agents are not wizards with magic wands. If a book project is worthy of being published, you can place it yourself with some persistence and confidence. If it's not up to par, no one will be able to sell it.

Publisher's Weekly once reported on an author who tried three different agents. Not one of them got her a book contract or even a magazine article sale (most agents will not handle article sales). One agent lost some of her work and did nothing to collect the percentage of royalties on a book the author sold herself.

Some authors with little confidence in agents have handled the contract and rights details for their books themselves and have done fairly well at it. Many others, however, have come out on the short end of the stick. It's a long proven fact that most agents usually get the author a much better deal and a higher advance. There is no question that the right agent can be a real help to an author. The top New York agents, for example, are in daily contact with most of the top publishers, often have lunch with leading editors, and have years to decades of experience negotiating book deals for authors.

When you reach the point in your writing that you feel the need for a literary agent to represent you, you can contact them and go from there. I recommend that you first have one or more manuscripts that you have done your absolute best on and believe are good enough to show a worthy agent. If you have some publishing credits behind you (any kind of writing credits at all – meaning articles, newsletters, anything that was published), you can then approach an agent. Wait until you have at least one completed book manuscript and be certain it's in the best shape possible. Then contact the agents of your choice.

What Agents Do for You

An agent I met years ago in New York, Donald MacCampbell (now deceased), gave some of the best advice to authors I have ever seen in his book, *The Writing Business*. It was my distinct pleasure to meet Donald, who was a gentleman first and literary agent second. I was just starting out, and found his advice very helpful. Some of the top agents won't give an author the time of day, but Donald took the time and interest to advise me on how to proceed.

Donald MacCampbell thought it was always best to personally meet an agent before signing up as a client. He put it this way: "You must try to meet an agent in person before you become involved, so that together you can assess the likelihood of a long-term relationship. It is very much the same as entering a marriage: you do not have to be in love, but had better be damn good friends."

Consider the future. If you intend to publish a number of books in the years ahead, the services of a literary agent are a must. You could lose a lot of money by trying to handle everything yourself.

However, if you plan only a book or two, you may be able to handle things yourself, after gaining knowledge of the business and preferably some skill in the art of contract negotiation.

Other Benefits of an Agent

Still other sensible reasons for working with an agent, assuming you can find the right one for you, include the following:
- Your agent can encourage you when things are not going well.
- Your agent can explain confusing clauses in a book contract and sometimes get you a better deal. This is especially true for the subsidiary rights split between your publisher and you, the author.
- An agent may well become a friend and someone you can check with regarding new ideas for future books.
- Your agent can see to it that you get the best possible royalty rate, whether for a hardcover, trade paperback, or standard paperback.

A great many authors believe that it's absolutely crucial for an author to have an agent if the book involved is fiction. Many authors are able to sell nonfiction books on their own by dealing directly with publishers. Even so, a worthy agent can usually get an author a better nonfiction deal. The question of the ability to negotiate comes into play here.

Generally speaking, authors should write and not get into negotiating. For one thing, the author is "too close" to the deal since it's his or her book project. This is not to say that authors cannot turn out to be great negotiators, but this is not usually the case.

If and when you deal with the powerhouse New York publishers, I believe you would fare better with a worthy agent in your corner. There is a kind of "star list" of top New York agents, but they are tough to reach in many cases. It's well worth trying if you believe your book deserves a star type agent to represent it, just keep in mind that you may never hear back from them, and most may not even respond at all. This, however, can vary at different times of the year. Some of these star agents (and note that I said only *some*) have grown used to extreme power within their field, so tread softly and do not test their patience and kindness in communicating with you, if in fact they do.

You must also keep in mind that certain agents have hundreds and hundreds of author clients, so it may be several months before you hear back from them regarding their yes or no decision about representing you. This would be after they first agreed to consider your project.

How to Get a Good Agent to Represent You

Ordinarily, you will want to seek out an agent no later than after signing your second book contract. Many professionals feel that an author should go for an agent after a first book sale. However, there's no guarantee that you'll get a good agent after the first, third, or twentieth book sale. Many of the top agents already have more clients than they can properly represent.

Get some bestsellers on your list, though, and many agents may well perk up with new interest. A "hot" author naturally has a wider choice of agents. After trying the better agents for years without success, many authors give up and simply continue to represent themselves. Quite a few do well on their own and later wonder why they spent so much time and effort seeking an agent. Others feel throughout their careers that they would have done much better if only they had been represented by a heavyweight, top caliber New York agent.

The Three Best Ways to Get an Agent

1. As already discussed, e-mail or snail mail the agent of your choice and ask if he or she will read and consider your manuscript or outline – synopsis plus chapters.

2. Travel to New York (the "Mecca" of the book publishing world), LA, Chicago, or wherever your agent is located, but write to the agent first and request an appointment. You must be able to convince the agent in your letter (or e-mail) that seeing you will be worth their time. If you have a very commercial book to pitch (hopefully), then describe it in your letter or e-mail, but just enough to arouse interest and curiosity. Whet the agent's interest and appetite for your book.

3. Pick up the telephone and call the agent's office. Tell whoever answers the phone who you are, where you're calling from, and why. Some lucky authors have actually landed very good agents this way. Needless to say, they either called at the right time, or the agent simply happened to be accepting new clients at that particular time. Watch out with this method. The large majority of agents do not want phone calls. They much prefer your communication to be by letter, whether it's snail mail or e-mail. Why antagonize them from the beginning with a phone call?

Let me add here that a few agents do not mind a phone call. The late Scott Meredith, who was a top New York agent for many years, truly liked his authors. In fact, he gave his home phone number to each new client and took calls from some of his authors in the middle of the night. Meredith encouraged me way back when I was starting, and he always responded promptly to mail. Far from simply being an effective literary agent, he was also a good person.

A Smart Way to Get an Agent

One smart way to snag an agent is to sell a book project yourself and then dangle the deal in front of the agent of your choice. This method often works well because it offers the agent tempting bait. In return for his attention and acceptance of you as an author client, you drop a book sale in his (or her) lap and thus a commission (the agent's commission) of the advance and resulting royalties earned by your book.

Many agents still find it hard to turn down such a sure thing. It may depend on which publisher your book is going to be with and what that particular agent thinks of both your book and that publisher.

Mary Roberts Rinehart was once reported to be the highest paid author in America, and she always worked without an agent. If she was still writing today, she would probably be all too happy to be represented by a quality agent.

If your books deserve to be published, there are editors waiting to read them. These same editors may, at times, suggest worthy agents to you. Some editors will do this while others would not even think of it. Just always keep in mind that there will probably always be some editors out there who will recognize the value of your books and act accordingly. So if you never land an agent, simply represent yourself. The main thing, no matter what, is to go on writing.

Whichever way you go, with or without an agent, always know that you can find a publisher if the book is right. Focus on writing the best books you can. With a few mini-bestsellers to your name, or a track record of published credits, perhaps some worthy agents will contact you. At that point, you can sign with the one you like best and believe would be the most effective in representing you. Or you may decide to continue going it alone, as many happy and successful authors have done.

9
Getting Along With Editors

❖ ❖ ❖

Many an author wisely attempts to sell a book to an editor before very much of the manuscript is completed. Therefore, knowing how to get along with editors can be vital to your success. This chapter is meant to save you time, misunderstanding, frustration, and money in dealing with various editors.

Much of the information is based on direct experiences I've had over a period of several decades. There are good and poor editors, responsible and careless ones, courteous and rude ones, and professional and not-so-professional ones.

Whether you write novels or nonfiction, you'll have to deal with editors until the day you get an agent. Even then, you will still deal with editors. Many authors want to keep up with what's going on with their book projects. Direct communication with editors makes that possible and often sooner than with agents.

Many authors have done well using an agent to represent them rather than contacting editors themselves and acting as their own agent. There are advantages and disadvantages to either choice. Certainly today's fiction author is heading for deep water without an agent's representation.

The best advice I can give you about agents is to carefully check them out before signing up as a client. There are high quality agents, mid-quality, and low quality ones. Trust is an absolute must in the author-agent relationship. The wrong agent can be a big drag on your career and can short-circuit the success you seek.

In most cases, an agent won't even consider taking you on as a client until you've had one or more books published. So you will typically be representing yourself, at least in the beginning. Here are a number of realities about editors that you should keep in mind for better overall results in working with them:

- In spite of upwards of 65,000 new books being published each year, many editors are still looking for fresh projects.
- Many editors move around frequently from publisher to publisher in an effort to both advance their careers and earn more money. A number of them play "musical chairs." If your editor leaves in the middle of your book getting through the publishing process, it can dash the chances for your book getting a good start. Obviously, the editor you've worked with is the main advocate and champion for your book. No one else at the publishing company cares about your book like the editor you worked with and know.
- Generally speaking, editors earn less money than agents, but this depends on which ones you're talking about. Editors at big publishing houses may well earn a lot more money than small and one or two person agencies in various parts of the nation.
- Editors appreciate receiving a query describing your book project before the proposal or manuscript is sent. In fact, in today's business, most editors prefer a synopsis – outline and several chapters. This saves the editor's and author's time.
- Some editors don't like simultaneous submissions (contacting a bunch of editors at the same time about your new project).

Other editors do not mind if you let them know that fact upfront. Some publishers – via their editors – may occasionally ask for an exclusive look for a set period of time.
- The majority of book editors are overworked, are forced to attend too many meetings, and have to face all sorts of deadlines. Show them that you understand their time constraints and don't bug them. They will then remember you favorably and want to work with you again in the future.

Pressures on Authors

Authors also face pressures, including deadlines, finding quality agents and editors to work with, locating the right publishers who won't let their books come into the world "stillborn," and of course the hard work of writing the best nonfiction book or novel possible.

In today's world, the wise author knows that he or she must do everything possible to promote the book, and that means getting radio and television interviews if at all possible, publicity, lecture tours, promotion tours, bookstore visits, autograph sessions, and anything, everything else to increase sales. In this computer age, many publishers even expect the author to have his or her own website, blog, or both for more promotion. Some editors and agents even refer to it as "the author's platform," a new phrase that has been added to the author's pressure line in the 21st century. In fact, a number of editors and agents won't even consider a new book unless the author can prove the "expected platform" for sales is there.

In other words, creating a strong book is just the beginning. All these other related tasks must be taken into account; in truth, today's author must wear more "hats" than at any other time in publishing history, at least in my opinion. Some of the more demanding (and sometimes arrogant) editors and agents expect the author to map out the competition any new book will face, come up with the greatest marketing plan, and submit a list of every book with any remote similarity that has come out since the end of the 19th century. Oops, I'm stretching it a bit on that last one, but you get what I mean. Gone are the days when just writing the best book possible was enough. Today's author has to be prepared for every eventuality or not even step up to the plate.

Notes From a Big Name Author

A "blockbuster" name author (I know some of the nicer ones) told me not long ago that he has yet to find a genuine ongoing relationship with a publisher or agent. "You're a number to many publishers," he says. It's very difficult to become friends with some editors or agents, so don't go out on a limb to win them over. You may get chopped off quickly. Strive to be as businesslike as possible. On the other hand, some editors and authors become friends after dealing with each other for years. Friendship with an editor is a possibility, then, but a remote one. Don't count on it.

One of the nicest editors I ever met was Doubleday's Ken McCormick, who edited the books of early presidents of the United States and a lot of other bestsellers. He was always nice, warm, and entirely professional. He encouraged me with my writing, was very helpful with advice, and told me some of the greatest stories in publishing history. We shared some great New York lunches, and Ken even took me to some top Manhattan restaurants as his guest, as did a number of other fine editors, and also some agents.

Remember this. From the viewpoint of many authors, simply replying and communicating with the author promptly wins his or her respect for that editor. This is especially true for editors at major publishing houses in New York, London, Toronto, Paris, and other key centers.

What else do editors do to command respect? The ones who are able to see the potential of a given book, whether nonfiction or fiction, will sometimes make very helpful suggestions for changes such as a different chapter format, a new slant, or other ideas that the author may not have even considered.

Make no mistake that, like authors, editors can make mistakes. I once sat in a Doubleday editor's office discussing a proposed novel. The editor said, in a polite way, that the idea, material, and even the title were "outside the Doubleday ballpark." Imagine my surprise to see, just a year later, the exact same title and idea in a published novel (by another publisher), in the stores. Coincidences of course do happen. Needless to say, I was still surprised. My point is that some editors have more vision and can grasp idea potential better than others. The same is true for agents.

Those editors who view themselves as advocates for the books in their houses are usually very professional. In other words, the editors who get an author's book through the publishing process, and do it smoothly and on time, are valued and respected by authors.

When a book needs revision, an editor can offer advice and direction for an author, but given the hectic schedule of many editors, this guidance may be limited to certain, or special, authors whose books are the lead titles for a given publishing season.

Editors who believe in authors and their books are highly valued and appreciated. Legendary author James Michener often stated how helpful his editor was on various books, as his work usually needed to be heavily edited.

Some Special Advice

You must absolutely keep in mind that bad-to-dreadful economic periods affect the publishing business just like other industries. Just keep the faith that "this, too, will pass." Once again, always remember what Isaac Asimov said: "The book will always be with us. Even in bad economic periods people will continue to buy books." Bennet Cerf, the founder and genius of Random House, said the same thing. Asimov also emphasized the portable quality of the book. "You can take a book almost anywhere – the beach, on a plane, and most other places." I believe there is something warmer, more personable, about holding a physical book rather than lugging a laptop around. And while devices like Amazon's Kindle are even lighter than some books, such technology is still less friendly and companionable than a well-loved bound book.

In trying to give you the full picture, I must warn you about a grisly truth regarding the publishing industry. Editors are swamped by e-mails from authors all over the map. This has unfortunately created a situation most authors describe as "the no-reply editors problem."

Frankly, there is much more of this going on today than back in the less hectic twentieth century. Before e-mail became the preferred form of communication, it may have taken *longer* to hear back from an editor via snail mail, but my experience was that nine out of ten editors *always* replied (using the self-addressed stamped envelope provided by the author).

It's a different game today. Editors receive many e-mail queries as well as snail mail query letters. Add that to all the meetings and details each book requires, and you get a small idea of how swamped they are. Bear all this in mind. Try to put something in the subject line of your e-mail query that will persuade or urge the editor to respond.

There are other claims too. I once heard one northeast author claim that "some New York editors like to deal with authors they already know and perhaps socialize with." Maybe this is true in a few cases, but I still personally think that the great majority of editors do their very best to give every author a fair chance, providing they are truly interested in the book being pitched. The point here is to realize that rejection on one level or another is inevitable. A real author just accepts the fact that this will happen and perseveres. Like Sinatra's great recording, "That's Life," simply pick yourself up, dust yourself off, and get on with your writing career. Move on to other editors. If an editor *never* responds to your queries, cross him off your list. There are always others who will communicate with you.

Fortunately, I've been blessed to have worked with some excellent book editors over my three decade career – and still counting. When visiting New York, Chicago, or LA, editors have taken me to lunch, always been happy to discuss new or current projects, and treated me with the utmost professionalism. This has been true for large, medium, and small publishers.

Many New York editors today prefer to deal through a literary agent, so please keep that in mind. For the foreseeable future, the power agents rule. If you are unable to land a star agent, don't let it keep you from writing. Life does go on, and it's not the end of the world. I've worked with and without agents. I admit it's true that the top powerhouse agents can get you a better deal, but they are tough to land. Some authors refer to the top agents like they are gods, but the ones I've met and dealt with (mostly New York) were very fair and honorable. There are some bad apples in every barrel. Some of them can be rude, but so can authors and editors at times – like all people.

There are many very good agents who may not be in the top 10 or 15 list, but you can work well with them. There are also many quality agents in other locations than New York or Chicago, so remember that too. Some authors move around, switching from one agent to another. If you achieve some bestselling books, don't be surprised if you start hearing from them. The incredible thing about my own career was the fact that very early in my writing, a New York star agent, considered by many to be in the top three or four, invited me to New York to discuss signing a book. I had never heard of them at the time, so I declined. Dummy me, but I was very busy and could not at that time take off for New York. What I'm saying to you is that anything can happen.

My Final Word on Editors

Before ending this chapter, please write this in red letters and place it in your favorite notebook or somewhere you will be sure to see it every single day. I call it the truth of all truths in this publishing business: *Nobody, no agent, publisher, editor, or author, really knows for certain where the next blockbuster book may surface.* Some guess and think they know, but nobody knows for sure. The same thing is true for new movies. Nobody, no matter how experienced, can predict the future.

      I hope this chapter will prove to be helpful to you as you launch into your own writing career or escalate it. I like to think that the books I wrote for authors will go on helping them for years to come. Hang in there with your career – no matter what – and you will indeed make your mark.

10
Research and Interviews Add Depth

❖ ❖ ❖

Whether you choose to write a novel or a nonfiction book, a must for your manuscript is research. It's a vital ingredient for producing a worthy book. Good research material brings books to life, and thoughtful and imaginative research lets the reader know that the author has done his or her homework. The resulting book has substance and value.

The Benefits of Research

- You uncover important facts for your project.
- Your finished book is more significant and up to date.
- The result of important research can mean a greater demand for your book. The new information you present may have a far-reaching influence on readers.
- The right kind of research helps an author to sense what must be said in the book.
- The research some authors do for historical novels, for example, can help put their books on the bestseller lists.

- Many authors have come across ideas and material for their next books while doing original research.
- Researching for a book is fascinating for many authors. Some hate it while others love and thrive on it. One pitfall is spending too much time on research, making it an end in itself. Don't fall into this trap.
- Research has power. It adds color, interest, accuracy, reality, believability, and the stuff of life itself to novels and nonfiction books.

How to Plan and Organize Your Research

Here are some guidelines on doing research for the book (or books) you're now planning to write. The list is by no means complete. If you're new to research, your librarian can be a big help.

- Some very useful research tools that you will want to have on hand for your writing include *Elements of Style*, the *Chicago Manual of Style*, and *Words into Type*.
- The internet is a natural and marvelous research tool for authors. The internet's arrival on the world scene was like a great gift dropped into the hands of authors everywhere. With the internet in today's world, authors no longer have to go to libraries to do much of their research, unless they wish to do so. Today they can sit at home and do an amazing amount of research via the internet, assuming they have a home computer. Even without a home computer, authors can use a library computer (though usually for only a limited time period, so others may use the same machine).
- You may find it interesting to see what other books are being published. *Books in Print* gives you an ongoing and continuous list of the new books coming out each year. This research source is very helpful in seeing what other books have been published on the subject you are considering writing about either now or in the future.

- Some authors take notes while reading and record them on index cards for later reference. Others like to use notebooks or large yellow or white legal pads.
- Begin your book project with some background reading. If you're writing a novel, for example, read about the period of time you plan to use, i.e., the Civil War, World War II, the Victorian period in England, the eighteenth century, and so on. If your book is nonfiction, read for a general knowledge of the subject (books, encyclopedias, and magazine and newspaper articles). Some books will be more useful than others, so choose your selections carefully.
- For novels, especially historical ones, you will find it useful to make a list or sketch of the key events in which you want your characters involved.
- For nonfiction books, be sure to read other published books on the subject, both old and new ones, along with articles in booklets, newspapers, and magazines.
- For both novels and nonfiction books, diaries, old letters, and dated articles can prove to be very helpful. Even old weather reports have helped various authors at times.
- When you have decided on the place and time of your novel (if your project is fiction), you will find that certain biographies and histories of the era paint a good picture. They can be of great use.
- Diaries of the specific period you're writing about can be especially helpful. They help an author to add details, including what people were thinking about at that time, the politics and customs, fashions, the popular songs or books of the time, and more.
- Don't forget research institutes. Most countries have them, and they may be able to provide you with some key information.
- Old documents and letters, as mentioned, may be good sources of facts for a variety of books.

- Personal interviews remain one of the best ways to get material for a book. People themselves are an endless source of material.
- If at all possible, you should visit the locale you are writing about, for this method can lead you to useful facts and information inaccessible through more remote means.

Finally, remember: many people are flattered by an author's request for an interview, though some don't like to see a tape recorder during the session. You can ask them upfront if they mind the use of a recorder, but if they indicate no, you're left taking notes the old-fashioned way. If this is the case, try to get down what they tell you as accurately as possible.

Personal Interviews Add Freshness

Some of the best material for your book can come from personal interviews. Keep this special source in mind and try to line up the interviews you want in plenty of time, so that you will have the notes from them ready when it's time to start writing your book.

One interview I was fortunate enough to obtain from a major Hollywood songwriter became the basis for one of the strongest chapters in my first published book on songwriting. I spent about four hours on two separate days in the home of a talented film songwriter and winner of three Academy Awards. It was the most fascinating interview I had done to date, and the material from the interview made a fine chapter on songwriting for motion pictures.

If you wish to interview some celebrity for your book, you may have to contact the person's manager or public relations agent. From that point on, you may or may not be granted an interview, depending on the person's schedule, your own credentials, the nature of what you're writing, and other factors.

Some celebrities and key people you may want to interview can be contacted directly by mail – though this has gotten tougher in recent years. They may agree to an interview, depending on what your e-mail or letter says, your background, where the material will be used, and if they can fit the interview into their busy work schedule. Be sure to mention anything you have had published in your letter, including articles you've done, books, or booklets. That may help you get the interview.

Prepare for Every Interview

Before you interview anyone – and especially anyone well-known or important – be sure you have done your homework. Read about the person, know the key facts about his or her life, and consult newspaper or magazine indexes for further information. This advance reading will help you during the interview and make it go more smoothly.

It is also very useful to have a list of the questions you want to ask during each interview, whether the person you interview is famous or not.

Who's Who contains the basic facts about well-known people. Many specialties (like science, writing, and historical personages) have their own special directories and your librarian can help you to find the ones you need to consult.

Author John Brady has written a very helpful book titled *The Craft of Interviewing*. This book can guide you in all facets of conducting a successful interview.

Once again, if and when you use a tape-recorder during an interview, be sure it's working properly. Accuracy, as already stated, is vitally important. Statements people make can be, and are, sometimes taken out of context. Learn to be a fair and accurate interviewer. You will be considered a real professional if you do.

11
When It's Time to Start Writing

Bringing a book to life is exciting. Keep that point sharp in your mind. You're bringing something into the world that was never here before – a book authored by you. (Or it's the next new book written by you.)

Creating a book out of nothing is a wonderful experience. Whether it sells a million copies or only a few thousand, there is something very satisfying and even mystical about bringing a new book into the world. It's a one-on-one experience. It's *your* words and ideas and thoughts being transmitted to the minds and hearts of readers you will never meet personally. Yet in the pages of your book, you do meet the reader. You, as the leader or storyteller, take the reader on a journey beginning on page one and ending at the last sentence.

Many writers think about this before starting a new book. They ask themselves some key questions such as: How can I say what I want to say without boring the reader? How can I make the reader care about my characters and the situations they're involved in? How can I entertain or instruct the reader in this book? These are important questions to ask before writing word one of your book.

Don't Let All That Material Scare You

Most writers never forget the experience of writing their first books, and many never lose their sense of pride or enthusiasm for their first published work. Whether the book you want to write is your very first or your thirtieth, don't let all the material you've gathered for your book scare you.

Some authors collect wheelbarrows of material for a book. When they're ready to start writing, they pile all the notes on their desk, or spread it out all over their office, room, table, apartment, condo, or whatever. Then they sit there for days just staring at that mountain of material.

If you worry about how you're going to get all your notes and material into the pages of a full-length book, you will constantly be on edge. Here are some specific ways to view all the material you've gathered when you're ready to start writing:

- You don't have to use the entire mountain of notes, just the very best of what you've found.
- If you already have an outline, you will have a framework showing where the material will be used.
- You can soon make your mountain of notes much smaller by dividing it into the key parts of your book. This process will become clear to you by simply sorting through the material.

Get a handle on the beginning, middle, and ending of your book. Then that mountain of notes you first had in front of you will have dwindled to a molehill, or at least a smaller mountain.

Break Your Material Down into Sections

One of the best ways to get organized for the actual writing is to break down the mass of notes and material you have into sections. Some authors like to use three-by-five cards for taking notes. When you've finished your research, group the cards according to key sections. This basic method, with variations, seems to work for many writers.

You may use other methods to break down your material, such as file folders or large envelopes to hold all the notes and material for major sections of your book.

After you've divided the material into sections, you will usually find that the task of writing looks easier. One reason is that you no longer have a huge mass of material. You can see the various sections of your book and the material for each one.

Some writers simply file their notes and research information into three key sections – the beginning, the middle, and the end – and go on from there. Others like to use more sections. You will have to experiment to find out what methods work best for you.

Chapters Will Fall into Place

If you don't already have an outline prepared for your book chapters, the various sections into which you divide your material will often suggest chapter divisions.

In other words, your sections will become chapters. Whatever heading you use for a section may be a natural chapter heading, or at least offer some hints for the title.

Now you can see why having a list or outline of your book chapters is helpful: you merely place the material you've obtained under each chapter. This system allows you to line up the material for each chapter of your book. When you are ready to start writing, you simply pull out the material for that chapter and you're in business. Do the same for every chapter until you've completed your project.

There are other methods of organization, but this one is as good as most. You may find that you're the type of author who just prefers to pile all your notes in one place and then start writing.

Maybe so, but a lot of authors like to break down the initial block of material into smaller, key sections. Remember, chapters make a book. It's comforting for an author to know that the material for each succeeding chapter is ready and waiting to be used. This system keeps you enthusiastic and helps you write. It has worked well for me.

Plan the Best Writing Schedule for You

If you hold down a nine-to-five job, it's obvious that the only time you can spend on your writing is either early in the morning or later in the evening. You will need some time for recreation and relaxation, so try different schedules to find your best hours for writing.

Maybe you could get in two hours of writing in the morning before going to work. Thousands of authors like the early hours when their minds are fresh. Or you could work from eight or nine at night to midnight.

Try to put in three hours a day at your writing, if at all possible. If there is no way you can do this, then settle for an hour in the morning or evening. Many books have been written by authors who had only an hour or less a day to devote to their writing.

It's important for some people to write at the same place and at the same time each day. The mind becomes used to the routine and cooperates better than it would if you wrote at a different time and place each day – though even this is no problem for other authors. Many authors out there have the ability to write no matter where they are or what time of day or night it happens to be. I've seen writers at work on airplanes, subways, cruise ships, and lots of other places.

Some authors work hard Monday through Friday and then relax over the weekend. Others work the same hours at their writing desk six or seven days a week. There's a lot to be said for getting the first draft down on paper fairly quickly. This can be especially true when the book is a novel.

A long break from writing may cause difficulty in getting started again. There are natural rhythms in writing. This is one reason why many authors like to work every day when working on a book. A week or two away from writing, or even a weekend, may interrupt your normal rhythm.

Writing Discipline Gets Results

Before you fall asleep at night, it helps to think about the next day's writing session. Your mind will often work out the best way to handle the next day's material.

The writing you do each day pays off in a number of ways.
- The next scene for your novel may fall into place in your mind the night before, or you may wake up knowing just how to handle it.
- The momentum you've established keeps you enthusiastic.
- It has been said that a real author is one who enjoys realizing how many new pages were completed for a given day or week. Writing discipline keeps those pages piling up.
- Writing discipline helps enormously in getting more books completed.

One has to admire an author like France's George Sand, who I mentioned earlier. She stuck to her goal of an amazing 30 pages a night, no matter what. There must have been any number of nights when she did not feel like writing, was upset about something, sad, lonely for her children, or tired. But her goal was of prime importance to her. She absolutely refused to go to bed before writing her set number of pages. That is wonderful, incredible discipline. She's a strong example of what discipline can do for authors.

George Sand, John O'Hara, Steve Allen, and many other authors preferred to write late at night. O'Hara, in fact, wrote all night long. Discipline can be vital to your growth and success as an author. Surprising though it may sound, there are authors who sign book contracts, receive and spend their advances, and then never complete the books. Publishers have been burned by such authors who never deliver a manuscript, so they naturally look for assurances that an author – especially if unknown to them – will actually finish the book.

An author may have every intention of completing the manuscript when a contract is signed. Yet without discipline it just may not work out that way. New authors must strive to develop discipline, for it can play a key role in leading them to success. Most veteran authors know the importance of discipline in their work. They learn how to become disciplined and keep it going for them. It pays off in being able to write books in greater quantity and of higher quality. Most authors fully intend to honor their contracts. Be absolutely certain that you honor every contract you sign and do all in your power to deliver the best manuscript you're capable of writing. This should almost go without saying. Discipline will help you rise in the publishing business; cultivate it.

12
Mining Ideas for Bestsellers

Bestsellers are written on all kinds of subjects, so it makes sense to take stock of the variety of book categories open to you. Here are most of the popular and leading ones:
- Popular Psychology
- How-To
- Money-Making
- Self-Help
- Hobbies, Arts, and Crafts
- Cookbooks
- Art-of-Living
- Business and Professional
- Travel
- Religious-Inspirational
- Marriage Books
- History
- Child Care/Parental Books
- Women's Special Interest

- Sex
- Health/Wellness
- Physical Fitness
- Humor
- Biography
- Novels

The list above is not complete, but it should give you a good idea of the variety of subjects open to you as an author. Ideas for books, both nonfiction and fiction, are endless.

Writing a book that may do fairly well is one goal. Creating a bestseller is another. Authors have finished their books just hoping that they might earn enough to justify their time and effort. Some first novelists have been pleased to see their books sell five thousand to ten thousand copies. Other authors aim much higher and shoot for the bestseller lists every time they start a new book.

There will always be authors who write for the sheer love of writing. Some even feel compelled to write. But most authors write for money and because they have something important to say. A lot of authors dream of their books hitting the *New York Times* bestselling list, being reprinted in paperback for an astronomical sum, and hearing one fine day that Hollywood wants to buy the film rights to their novel.

There's nothing wrong with wanting a bestseller. One or more will at least help to open the doors of major publishers, editors, and possibly New York agents in the business. A proven bestselling author like Tom Clancy or Stephen King is assured a huge advance before the first word of their new books is written. Their previous track records are solid gold in the field.

Timeless Subjects Make Bestsellers

A look at the bestselling titles of today and yesterday reveals a characteristic shared by many of them. This vital quality is timelessness. Books that have this wonderful trait remain just as interesting, helpful, or fascinating years later as they were when first published.

Such books like *Treasure Island, The Joy of Cooking, Gone With the Wind, The Swiss Family Robinson, Great Expectations, Wuthering Heights, Frankenstein,* and many others all have this special quality of timelessness. They will probably be read many years from now, assuming planet Earth is still intact.

I challenge you to a test of your own judgment of books. Most publishers announce their new titles twice a year, in the spring and fall. Keep up with these new books, as reported in *Publisher's Weekly* and other trade journals. Then choose the books you feel are most likely to become bestsellers. Select them from the titles alone or by looking the books over when they arrive in stores. Here are some good reasons for conducting such a test:
- It will show you that a book's timeless quality can help make it a bestseller.
- It helps to develop your judgment.
- It stimulates your thinking about subject possibilities for your own books.
- You will develop a greater awareness of various book categories.
- It puts you in the editor's or publisher's shoes by letting you decide which books will become bestsellers.
- It's fun to see how well you did in this test, by comparing your own list of star choices with the sales figures for the books.
- It keeps you thinking about bestsellers in general.

Some Clues for Spotting Bestsellers

Here are some pointers for recognizing possible bestsellers. A book that appeals to one or more of the dominant desires of most people has a strong chance of being a bestseller.

When you consider new book projects, try to focus on one that includes some of these universal desires.

The list that follows includes 29 of the dominant desires of the masses. Many seek vicarious fulfillment when they select books, and they can be influenced to buy a book providing it seems to appeal to some of these ardent desires. Here they are:

- To make money
- To be praised
- To escape physical pain
- To attract the opposite sex
- To have beautiful possessions
- To save money
- To be healthy
- To be in style
- To save time
- To be like others
- To satisfy one's appetite
- To gratify curiosity
- To avoid trouble
- To be an individual
- To be popular
- To be self-confident
- To be expressive
- To have security
- To protect one's reputation
- To avoid criticism
- To take advantage of opportunities
- To avoid effort
- To have more leisure time
- To have prestige
- To be comfortable
- To advance in social or business life
- To have influence over others
- To be more creative
- To be important

The more of these universal desires your book promises to fulfill, the better your chances are for a bestseller and quite possibly a star seller. The list is in no certain order, meaning those listed near the bottom are just as important, just as dominant with the masses, as those at the top.

From now on, every time you buy, read, or look at a book, think about these dominant desires most people have. Ask yourself these three questions:

1. How many dominant wants does this book reflect or offer help in fulfilling?

2. What are the specific dominant desires behind the book? Try to name them.

3. In what manner does the author try to fulfill his or her promise to the reader?

A key point to remember is that countless people the world over want to *improve* their lives in one way or another. If the books you write can help them to do this, to achieve their goals, you have moved a lot closer to the bestseller lists. I'm speaking mainly of nonfiction books, since it's this type of book that generally offers practical help and guidance. Novels are more likely to provide pure escape for readers.

Realities Regarding Bestsellers

- Always keep in mind that publishers and editors sometimes make mistakes. A number of top-selling books were first rejected one or more times. Remember the example of *Lust for Life*, the great novel by Irving Stone, that was rejected by seventeen major publishers. It went on to become an international bestseller, sold big time, and was even made into a movie using the same title.
- The public's fancy can change very quickly. You have just as good a chance to spot a trend developing as anyone else.

In fact, newcomer authors sometimes hit just the right time with refreshing new books.
- Remember throughout your writing career that word-of-mouth advertising has turned many a book into a blockbuster. It's a fact that people who buy and like a book tell their friends, neighbors, associates, and relatives about it. The word spreads and sales keep climbing. Get the potentially endless chain of word-of-mouth publicity going for your book, or at least do all you can to trigger it.
- If you can write a clear and effective sentence, and are willing to do the work involved in completing a manuscript, there is always the chance your book will make it through the publishing process in good shape and carve a worthy place for itself in the marketplace. A strong book and cover-jacket will help. Sometimes a new book is simply lucky and gets all the right breaks, has a lot going for it, some fortunate publicity and promotion behind it, and may then take off like a rocket. Yet never forget this truth: even with every bad break against them, some books defy the odds and still become bestsellers, amazing all the so-called experts in the process.
- Never underestimate the power of a strong title for a book. Publishers, editors, agents, and book buyers respond to great titles. Here are a few examples:
  - *Midnight in the Garden of Good and Evil*
  - *Chicken Soup for the Soul*
  - *The First Immortal*
  - *Why Bad Things Happen to Good People*
  - *Ten Stupid Things Women Do to Mess up Their Lives*
  - *Mutant Message Down Under*
  - *Parenting Isn't for Cowards*
  - *The Truth Machine*
  - *The Dark Side of Camelot*
  - *The Other Side of the Rainbow*

–*Driving Under the Influence*
–*Men are from Mars, Women are from Venus*

Never stop mining your own mind, background, knowledge, experience, and all other factors of your life for bestseller ideas. They are out there in your daily life and the world you live in year after year. Train your mind to be constantly alert for possible great

13
What About Length?

❖ ❖ ❖

Length for a book was mentioned earlier, but you may find more information on the subject useful. To estimate the length of your manuscripts, figure on about 250 words for each double-spaced, typed manuscript page for word-processors. You can obviously get a lot more words typed on a computer, depending on your margin width and font style, but typically a double-spaced computer-typed manuscript yields about 300 words per page.

Some Novels Dictate Their Own Length

It's usually a mistake to predict the length of a novel you plan to write. It may run much longer or shorter than you originally intended. Novels run from about 100 pages (often called novellas) to over 1000 pages. Family-saga-type novels usually run considerably longer than a general novel. You'll find the following calculations on various novel lengths helpful:

Fiction
General novels – 100 to 300 pages. Many run about 200.
Family sagas – 500 to 1,000 pages
Romances – 300 to 700 pages, more or less.
Adventure novels – 200 pages or more on the average
Mystery novels – about 200 pages or so.
Humorous and miscellaneous novels – 100 to 200 pages.

Nonfiction
Nonfiction books run from 100 pages or so up to 1,000 pages or more. *American Caesar*, the book on MacArthur by William Manchester, as an example, has 700 pages. Presidential memoir books can run over 1,000 pages.

Please bear in mind that today there's an overall trend toward shorter books.

Full Value for Their Money

The length of a book can have an influence on a buying decision. I've often watched browsers in bookstores examine the thickness of a book, either before or after noting the price.

People in general do tend to feel that a 25 or 30 dollar book should offer a suitable thickness. Book buyers in general seem to forget that it's not how many pages that are in a book that matter, but the content of those pages.

A well-known author may get away with a shorter book. The name recognition makes up for the price. The average book buyer thinks seriously before spending 25 dollars or more for a book. This is especially true during poor economic periods and recessions. Many business and professional books are priced over 35 or 40 dollars, so the size of these books is usually carefully noted in relation to the asking price. Buyers tend to feel that they are getting their money's worth if the book they're considering is thick in relationship to the price printed on the inside flap.

Short Books Are Bestsellers Too

Don't think that a book has to be 1,000, 900, or even 500 pages in order to become a bestseller. Short books have also done well and continue to do so. They will most probably continue to do well in the years ahead. Not all of them sell big of course, but some catch on every year and chalk up very respectable showings.

A number of book buyers evidently make their decisions to purchase a book on pure impulse. So if a given book strikes a browser's fancy, he or she may buy it, regardless of the length. *Acres of Diamonds*, for example, is a short book, but it has sold for many years. So have other short books, such as *How to Speak Southern, Don't Sweat the Small Stuff,* and *Return From Tomorrow*.

Length Usually Takes Care of Itself

The average length of most books is about 200 pages, more or less. A number of others run about 250 pages. This, of course, doesn't mean that a book of yours can't run 125 pages, 275, or over 500.

Each book tends to forge its own length. Just write until the story reaches a conclusion or your nonfiction book comes to a satisfying and logical ending.

Some Publishers Have Minimum Lengths

When you have a publisher in mind for one of your book projects, it's wise to check out any length requirements. You can find the publisher's requirements listed in the market books for authors published yearly (*Literary Market Place, Writer's Market*, and *The Writer's Handbook*).

Many of the listings state a minimum length of 50 thousand to 60 thousand words. One major publisher in the East wants nothing under 80 thousand words. Other book publishers are flexible, however, and may be willing to accept a shorter or longer length than that stated in the market information for their company.

The key point about length is that it's usually much easier to cut than to lengthen a manuscript at the last minute. This is especially true after a manuscript has been delivered to a publisher and the process leading to publication has begun.

A number of religious book publishers will take books of shorter length. I've seen many such books in recent years, and the length has often run about 20 thousand to 30 thousand words. Many others have a total length of 35 thousand to 40 thousand words. A religious or inspirational book can be only 100 to 125 pages and still sell many copies. Some seem to make their way into the book world regardless of their brevity.

Write Books of Various Lengths

If you plan to write more than one book in the future, a good general rule is to not limit yourself to any certain length. Shoot for a variety of book lengths.

Your first book might run about 150 pages. Your second one could be shorter or longer. In the course of your writing, you will probably do both long, short, and medium- length books. Just let each book lead the way. It's what you say on those pages that are important. So don't worry about the length of your book. Say what you need to say and then stop.

14
How Many Drafts Does It Take?

❖ ❖ ❖

The number of drafts needed for a well-written book depends on the author and the nature of the work. The majority of writers accept the truth that most books require some degree of revision. There just aren't too many authors who can sit down and turn out hundreds of pages of perfect prose. Rewriting is part of the trade.

Many years ago now, Rosemary Rogers, a prolific author of romance novels, rewrote *Sweet Savage Love* 23 times before sending it to Avon Publishers in New York. Her book became a big bestseller and sold millions of copies. The point is that revision can and does improve a manuscript. Few authors have the patience to rewrite over twenty times, but many who earn their living by the pen (or, nowadays, by the computer, to be more precise) believe in at least several revisions.

Ways to Revise Your Work

There are several methods of rewriting your manuscript. You'll want to try each one so you can discover which you prefer. These revision choices include the following:

- Do one or more complete rewrites of your manuscript.
- Change and correct your manuscript as you go along. In other words, make corrections on each page as you write it.
- After completing a first draft, go back over the complete manuscript, writing in all changes and corrections with a red pencil or pen. Then type a fresh copy.
- Write one or more chapters and then revise them before proceeding further with your book.

Some Books Turn Out Well With Slight Revision

Some authors do too much revising. They seem obsessed with reworking a manuscript and are never satisfied. There comes a point with every manuscript when it's time to let go of it and to send it on its way to market. Part of the reason some authors can't let a manuscript go is a fear that it won't sell or that it can still be improved.

Authors can get so close to a manuscript that it's like parting with a baby; they hate to say good-bye. Quite a few feel let down when they reach the end of a book. When you've done your level best on a manuscript and honestly believe that you can't improve it anymore, send it to a publisher. Then try to forget it. Turn to a new project. Better still, relax for a week. You deserve it. You've earned a break at that point.

Too much revision can ruin books. It's also true that books you may write in the future will call for less revision than others. If your strength lies in the novel, for example, you may need less (or more) revision in your fiction than on a nonfiction book. It could go either way.

In time, you will be able to trust your own instincts. Something will tell you that a manuscript you have completed needs a rewrite or that it should have two more drafts. At other times, you will be certain that book you have completed needs only some minor corrections. Just remember always that most books can usually be improved via revision and rewriting.

Bestsellers Take Revision

Just because you rewrite the work three or more times is no guarantee that you will have a bestseller. Still, the history of bestsellers (I recommend you check this yourself) indicates that a lot of them had a considerable amount of revision done on them. Thomas Wolfe, the famous North Carolina author who wrote *Look Homeward Angel* and other impressive novels first brought a "sea of words" to his New York Scribner editor Max Perkins. Working for some time, Perkins and Wolfe whittled that huge sea of words down to a workable novel. It was slow, tough work, but they got it done. Without the genius of Max Perkins, no doubt one of the greatest editors of all time, it's doubtful that novel would have become what it did.

Ways to Revise and Improve Your Novel

Here's a list of some ways that a book manuscript may be strengthened and improved. I've done some editing for publishers, and a lot for my own books, and these guidelines were the main ones I followed.

- Change long and confusing sentences to short, clear ones. This can help just about any manuscript.
- Cut out overly technical words. Replace them with simple ones.
- Make paragraph transitions smoother.
- Shorten paragraphs that are clearly too long. Break them up into short- and medium-length ones.
- Cut material in a novel that does not seem to move the story along (sections that go off in other directions).
- Rewrite material that is too wordy.

- Dialogue is important in a novel, but avoid too much of it. Otherwise, the entire book becomes all dialogue. Alternate the flow of dialogue with narrative and descriptive passages.
- Delete material that is repetitious. Don't repeat what you've already said unless you wish to especially emphasize a point.
- Get variety in your nonfiction books. Don't present the material in the same old way.
- Check to see that there are plenty of examples and anecdotes in your nonfiction books. More can usually be added, but be selective about them.
- Limit the use of dots and dashes.
- Rewrite sections that just don't ring true or that seem confusing.
- Correct grammatical errors, spelling, and punctuation.

As long as you write, you'll profit from revision. Bestselling author Irving Wallace once said something about revision worth remembering: "Even the most prestigious authors still sit by themselves, alone, applying the seat of the pants to a chair, and with their tortured psyches and numbed fingers write and labor. That's the name of the game – work patience, and revision." So hang in there and revise. Then revise some more and hang in there. Works well no matter how you say it, and every book you write will be all the better for it.

15
Writing the How-To Book

❖ ❖ ❖

The how-to book has really come into its own over recent years. People everywhere seem to be more aware of the passing of time, so they want to get more out of their short lifetimes. How-to books have a wide appeal and often become strong sellers. Many of them become backlist titles and go on selling for years.

How-to books cover just about all areas of life today. Their sales can go way up during bad economic eras and uncertain times. Just name a subject; chances are good there's a how-to book on it. One major bookseller, Barnes and Noble, has estimated that how-to books account for about 30 percent of trade book sales.

My first published book was a how-to. I had been a published and recorded songwriter for years and had strong, firsthand knowledge about writing and selling songs. One day I just started a book on the subject. The resulting work did well in the marketplace and launched my journey into many other published books. Authors retain a special place in their hearts for their first book, and I still love that first one I did.

I learned even more about songwriting in the process of writing the book and got a great sense of satisfaction from doing it. As an added bonus, sales were very good for a first book at about 30 thousand copies. If you're very interested in a subject, as an author you are naturally going to do a better book on it. I had always loved the art and craft of songwriting, though I never thought I would one day write a book about it. About 30 more books were destined to follow that first one. It's been quite a ride through the publishing marketplace.

What You Need to Know About the How-To Book

- Stay aware of the variety of subjects available to you via the how-to book.
- If at all possible, locate and talk to authorities on the subject, even if you're one yourself. With their permission, put what they tell you into your manuscript. It will add weight and credibility to your book.
- The readers of how-to books want to know how something is done. Tell them in a clear, simple, and interesting way.
- Query publishers (and agents) first with a description of the project. You would also be smart to see if the publisher you have in mind has any how-to titles on his list. That publisher may have recently done a similar book. Some publishers do more how-to books than others, so do your research homework and check them out first.
- The subjects that interest you personally may make good how-to books. What do you know best? What are some of your strong interests? What can you do well? Special hobbies or talents might result in an idea. Sit down and list the subjects you already know a lot about and go from there.
- The more knowledge of and experience with a given subject you have, the more convinced an editor will be that you could do a good job on a book. So emphasize your skill or

background on the topic. Publishers and agents are looking for authors with the credentials to write how-to books on a variety of subjects. The book industry is going through changes, but good how-to books will continue to be published. If you happen to already be an experienced author with published credits, then you might think about writing a how-to book as a new project.

- Both paperback and hardcover publishers buy how-to books. Some publishers will issue such books in both formats or do it as a trade paperback rather than a small size paperback.
- Your enthusiasm as an author for a how-to subject is often the first step in writing a book on it. I have to really be interested in a subject before I even consider making a book about it.
- When you prepare a sample chapter or two for your how-to book, be sure to be specific enough. Your sample material must help sell an editor on your book.

Once again, publishers' preferences come into play. Some publishers will take a new book on a how-to subject already covered by their firm. In other words, they may already have a how-to on a certain topic but simply want another book on the same subject. Checking a publisher's catalog will help you a lot in deciding if they might be the right home for your book. Some publishers like to have several books on the same subject. In my own opinion (and many authors I've talked with agree), some large publishers come out with too many books on the same subject at certain times. Prentice-Hall, for example, once published about a dozen books on the subject of sales-marketing. When that is done, it hurts all the books published on the subject because they compete with each other. The resulting sales of each book are thus reduced. Yet some publishers insist on using the shotgun approach to publishing. This is one sound reason why a number of authors prefer to work with medium to small publishers. There is less chance of 10 or more books being published at the same time on the same subject. Many authors do books for both large and smaller publishers in the course of their careers.

Examples of How-To Books

Here are just a few examples of how-to books that generally did well in the marketplace. Notice the variety of subjects covered:
- *How to Be Your Dog's Best Friend*
- *How to Build a Real Estate Money Machine*
- *How to Improve Your Odds Against Cancer*
- *How to Get Your Child into Modeling and Commercials*
- *How to Develop Your ESP Power*

Ideas for How-To Books

From my own experience, I can vouch for the fact that ideas for new how-to books can come in a flash, or after a lot of thinking about new book projects you might like to do. Such ideas may occur to you at any time or place, so be ready. They may come from your own reading, experience, earlier jobs you had, or understanding of the needs, desires, and interests of people in general.

Here are some typical traits of an effective how-to book idea:
- It's an attractive, catchy, and/or up-to-date idea.
- The resulting book would have definite value for the reader.
- The project is worthy of being published, when ready, at this point in time.
- You, as author, are capable of completing the book and are enthusiastic about it.
- The idea has staying power. The finished book would have continuous appeal, helping it to sell for years to come.
- It's an idea that may reflect a current popular interest, trend, or event.

I believe an excellent example of all the above qualities for a very strong book is *Don't Sweat the Small Stuff*. Some might not think of it as a how-to book, but it basically tells the reader how to not be overwhelmed or knocked out of the box over the "small gritty details" that all humans go through.

How-to books, like all products, are subject to fluctuations of the market, but I personally believe there will always be how-to books. The appeal of this type of book could probably even be graphed to show its degree of popularity through the years and decades. You can prove this to yourself by looking through the catalogs of various publishers. You will notice how-to books on both their new and old lists.

Publishers learned way back that how-to books are a continuing backlist staple for them. Such books keep cranking out sales for them and royalties for authors. Many how-to books last much longer than the lead books that get all the plugs, publicity, and fanfare.

One author who specializes in this how-to category wrote four different how-to books in eighteen months. He also had three more similar books under contract and three others being edited. Not bad at all. It's true, however, that some authors have a natural feel and strong ability for this particular type of book.

Think Well About Writing a How-To Book

This kind of book offers you an excellent chance to sell your first (or tenth) book and see it in published form, either as a paperback, hardcover, or possibly both. Your enthusiasm in selling your first book could easily draw you into writing on a part-time basis and maybe later even full-time. Writing gets into your blood. Many authors simply could not stop writing even if they wanted to.

Think well about creating a how-to book. It's a good way to start a writing career. At this writing, with millions having lost their jobs due to the national meltdown, hordes of people are racking their brains and trying to "bounce back" by finding other work arenas and fields to enter. Do your first how-to book and you may well have a new – or second – career open up for you. It happens every day for new authors. There are hundreds of possible publishers, so you will always find writing work if you want it, assuming they like your book.

There is also another choice open to today's authors via electronic publishing where books are printed on demand and read online. Some of these e-book publishers pay larger royalty rates and even publish the book in the traditional form as well. This other way to publish is growing every year, so authors are not locked into going the traditional way to get their book into the market.

If you're seeking your first book credit, the how-to book can be your entrance into the fascinating business of books. If you already know your way around in the industry as an experienced, proven professional, the how-to book can add lots of nice green dollars (even though our current dollar seems to be going down the tube at present) to your bank account.

Read and write new how-to books for fun and profit. They can help you get started as an author and also help you become an established one – an author with a reputation for doing wonderful and well done how-to books.

16
Addicted to Romance

❖ ❖ ❖

There are two basic ways to get hooked on romance novels. One way is to read them, and the other way is to write them. Women authors usually have more interest in writing this type of book, but some men have done well at it too. As you might expect, women book buyers are the greatest fans, and it is a good idea to keep this audience in mind when writing romances. In fact, women dominate this field so much that reports of male authors using feminine pen names for their romances continue to circulate.

Women authors sometimes do amazingly well on their very first romance novel. There's a strong attraction for a woman who wants to write to try her hand at this type of book. Women who buy romances like plenty of action, lots of romance and generous amounts of sex, though there are other lines of no sex and sweet romance novels. This type of book also comes in categories like historical romance, contemporary, time travel, inspirational, and more.

The magic ingredients of love and romance are what millions of readers cannot resist. Many women book buyers have been shelling out money for this type of book all their lives. They're already hooked on buying romance novels. If the new ones they see in the bookstores (or online) seem to have these ingredients, many women will buy the books.

Dr. Joyce Brothers feels that love is the miracle drug of life. She once defined love as "having the same care and concern for someone else as you would have for yourself. Most people are not aware that you can make love last a lifetime." Part of the reason for the success of romance novels is the human desire for love and romance. A great many women all over the world never get enough of either in their lives.

These books transport their readers into a world of exciting romance, passion, and suspense. They forget their own troubles for awhile. They share, if only temporarily, the glamour of many of the settings and the ongoing experiences of the main characters of the book. They're in on the romance, love, and sex of the heroine.

There's no doubt that reading romance novels can offer release and escape for many women. It helps them to enter an exciting locale or setting – a fictional world – and to follow the character as she copes with her own set of problems, goals, and experiences. Women readers identify with the character's fulfillment and thus share in it vicariously.

There are strong reasons for believing that the romance novel will continue to sell in the years to come despite a glut of them in the current market. If you're a potential author, you should give some serious thought to writing this kind of book. You might do very well indeed on your first try. If you enjoy reading romance novels, so much the better. You already know the basic form for such books. If you haven't read too much in the field, read several books as you think about writing a romance novel of your own. Then try your hand at one yourself.

How to Get Ideas for Romance Novels

Cities and countries can be rich in ideas. Soak up some of the history of a particular city or country you would like to write about. Travel can also yield an abundance of ideas, and this does not mean that you have to go far away. Towns, cities, and other communities not far from you can lead to lots of ideas for romance novels, providing you keep your radar at the alert and your eyes plus ears open.

Here are some guidelines for getting ideas:

- Associations, meetings, and specialized societies may lead you to worthwhile ideas.
- Old legends may suggest wonderful romance novels.
- Play the game of what if. What if a certain character found herself caught up in a certain sequence of events? Experiment both on paper and in your mind. Turn ideas over regularly and consistently.
- Consider the gothic romance. Some of these types are still around, though they're not as popular as they once were.
- Items you read about anywhere can be a springboard to a book idea in this field.
- Read the published romance novels. They may suggest a locale, lead character, or era to you for a book you can write and sell.
- Your own memory may touch off a good romance novel.
- Old villages, battlefields, letters, scrapbooks, or anything may suggest a book. Shiloh, Vicksburg, and Gettysburg have all been featured locales. So was the Alamo in San Antonio, Texas, as well as various landmarks in England, France, Canada, Scotland, Australia, and other countries.
- The art of listening, conventions you attend, the conversations and remarks of others, their experiences, newspaper features and columns, television programs, and just living in general can all produce workable ideas for new romance novels.

Comments of Romance Authors

Barbara Ferry Johnson

Barbara, author of *Tara's Song*, believes that some paperbacks are now beginning to be thought of as good literature. "Women still buy magazines with little novels in them, but since the emergence of the affordable, varied paperback, they have turned more to them." They've actually been buying romance novels by the carload at various times.

Barbara does careful research for each of her books. "My books are not Gothic romances; the difference is that they are more period stories. There are love scenes, but I'm not clinically descriptive. And my heroines are not promiscuous. There's a difference between rape and seduction."

Lionors was Barbara's first novel, which was a period romance about King Arthur and a mysterious mistress by the name of Lionors. *Delta Blood* was her second. Set during the Civil War period in New Orleans, the book stayed on the *New York Times* bestseller list for eleven weeks.

Joan Wolf

Joan Wolf is an award-winning author of many romance novels. Some of her books include *Change of Heart, Beloved Stranger*, and others. One of her novels was "the passionate tale of Lady Barbara Carr's marriage to the handsome Virginian Alan Maxwell, initially so his wealth could pay her father's debts. Ultimately, she finds herself falling desperately in love with this colonial rogue."

Some romance novelists don't like to write explicit sex scenes. So they just leave them out, and their books are successful anyway. Others feel there must be some sex scenes in their novels, but they must be done in good taste and not explicitly. It's certainly possible to get emotion into these scenes, which is what women readers want, without being extremely detailed and explicit. It's true, too, that some authors in this field are capable of writing explicit scenes well, while others do poorly at it.

Patricia Matthews

Patricia Matthews has become a millionaire by writing a whole string of romance novels including *Love's Avenging Heart, The Birthright, Love's Raging Tide*, and others. The characters Patricia creates are usually complex people who scratch and fight their way through eras. They do strange things and get swept up in a variety of problems.

The romance novels of Patricia Matthews have happy endings. "Goodness triumphs in all of them; happy endings because that's what people want. That's one of the reasons they read them."

Matthews believes in strong villains and avoids repetition of two characters in the same situation book after book. She says that in the novel field, "All the stories have been written. It's the way the thing is put together that makes it different…if you succeed, that is."

The Barbara Cartland Formula

England's incredibly prolific Barbara Cartland used a basic plan. She started with a very handsome duke, marquis, or other titled hero who is haunted by some dark family secret. He meets a virginal penniless woman, and they fall in love. Some wicked relative is usually around, and there is a lot of period detail in the story. Cartland believed that "it's sweetness people crave."

Barbara Cartland lived like a queen on a 400-acre estate with servants and a string of secretaries to help her with her books. She dictated thousands of words daily and could turn out a new romance novel within a week or two. She wrote hundreds of published romance novels and no doubt still holds the record for the most published books in the romance field. She well deserved the title of Queen of Romance Novels.

Writing Your Own Romance Novel

Here are some guidelines for writing your own romance novel:

- Realize from the start that readers of this kind of book want escape. Make sure you provide it.
- Your main character will often emerge from the era or background you've chosen to write about. Live the life of your heroine in your mind. Identify with her as the story progresses.
- Make sure you have a strong theme for your novel before you begin. If you can express the theme to yourself in one simple sentence, so much the better.
- Develop a difficult situation for your heroine to face.
- The man in your heroine's life is a source of strength. He helps her to cope with a trying situation.
- Pick a day to make a start on your romance novel, whether it's doing research, planning and writing an outline, or completing the first page of the actual book.
- Set a goal of so many pages a day or week or so many chapters over a certain time. Then work toward that goal.
- Once you have about 50 pages and an outline, you can try to interest an agent or editor. Be sure to e-mail or write first for an okay to send your material, rather than just mailing or e-mailing it to them cold. If it's expected, it's more likely to get some quicker attention and a reply about it sooner. Most editors (and agents) want to see a query first.
- Strive to make the dialogue in your romance novel ring true. Does it sound right for your characters? A lot of your book will be dialogue.
- Rewrite those parts of your manuscript that need it.
- Don't give up if one, two, or a dozen publishers reject your novel. The next one you try might well accept it. Keep trying. Remember, the example of Rosemary Rogers and her

23-times-rewritten novel. Her persistence paid off, and she went on to great success in the field.

Don't believe that you can't write a romance novel if you hold down a nine-to-five job. One author, John Erskine, wrote his first bestseller by working just two hours a night for five months. The finished book was *The Private Life of Helen of Troy*. During the day Erskine handled a full university schedule.

Take this tip from successful romance novelist Rosemary Rogers: "Research is a compulsion with me." So spend time on your novel. Most successful romances are not turned out quickly. Some authors spend a year or more just in the research stage. This type of book has been very good to many authors, mostly women, and some have become rich from their books. You just might do the same one day and join their elite group.

In the words of a top New York agent, "It's better to discover your forte, concentrate on it so as to be type-cast. This is the type of author headed for the big time." In other words, "A successful author is known for a certain kind of story or type of writing." If the romance novel is your kind of book, I hope you build a solid reputation in this field. And may your first romance novel be a bestseller. But any book that you write and sell to a publisher is a real achievement. And you will know it when you see your book in print – your very first romance novel a reality. Go for it.

17
Writing a Religious-Inspirational

There will always be markets for religious-inspirational books. During tough economic times, wars and rumors of wars, and not-the-greatest eras in general, the sales of these types of books can rise. Why not try your writing ability in this category?

It seems certain that religious-inspirational books will be strong and continue selling for many years to come. One basic reason is the fact that multi-millions of people believe the world is moving toward some climactic and momentous event.

The point is that the time is *always* ripe for all kinds of religious and inspirational books. There may be one or more books ahead for you if you choose this category. In my own career, I have done several of them, and it means a lot to an author when a grateful reader takes the time to write and say that such a book helped them, inspired them, or influenced them to get through a trying time in their life.

General Religious and Inspirational Books

Numerous books fall into the religious or inspirational category. They may not be purely evangelical, as many define it, but they're still books that uplift the human spirit, provide light along life's way, and point to the eternal values of love, beauty, hope, faith, and wisdom.

Such books are often based on the personal experience of the author, or they give insight into various ways of coping with life's problems. Here are a few examples:

- *In His Strength*
- *The Christian's Secret of a Happy Life*
- *The Illustrated Gospel of John*
- *The Late Great Planet Earth*
- *Raising Positive Kids in a Negative World*
- *True Fellowship*
- *The Bright Side of Depression*

There are times when religious-inspirational books will far outsell the widely reported bestsellers. Those who compile various bestseller lists usually don't check with religious bookstores. This is why a number of top-selling religious books don't show up on such lists.

The Importance of the Religious Market

Evidence continues to grow that secular publishers are increasingly realizing the importance of the religious market. More secular publishers have been present at recent Christian booksellers' conventions than earlier events. A study conducted by Knowledge Industry Publications cited a trend that has had a favorable influence on religious book sales, namely, the aging of the population. Those in the 25 to 44 age bracket are big buyers of religious books. Their number is expected to increase by more than 10 million in the coming years.

Some religious books sell over a million copies. One book alone, *The Living Bible*, sold over 20 million copies in the same time period. In the words of a Doubleday editor, "one of the fastest-selling books that publisher has ever had was *Angels: God's Secret Agents* by Billy Graham."

All of this should convince you that the future for religious-inspirational books is a bright one. Now is the time to write such a book of your own.

How to Write and Sell the Religious-Inspirational

1. Query a likely religious-inspirational publisher after requesting the catalogs of a number of companies and studying their lists so you get an idea of the books they are doing. Word Books is one of the largest such publishers. Baker Books and Moody Press are two long-time publishers in this category.

2. Briefly describe the book you have in mind, explaining why you believe it would be a worthy addition to their line and what competing books there are on the subject. Include a working title for your book if possible. You should also ask if you may send an outline and one or two sample chapters.

3. If you get a green light to send your project, e-mail or snail mail your outline and sample chapters to the editor who has expressed interest in your book.

4. Then be patient. As a rule, religious publishers take longer to reach a decision than a number of secular companies. You should be prepared to wait for six weeks to several months. A literary agent can often get you faster decisions, but generally speaking religious publishers take longer to decide.

5. When you first contact a publisher, it's helpful to ask how long they take to report back on a project sent to them. If you don't wish to wait up to several months, you can try some other publishers. It naturally takes longer for an editor to respond to a finished manuscript or even a partial one than to an outline and chapter or two. They need time to read a complete manuscript.

6. Remember that some religious publishers require a complete manuscript before they will consider publishing your

book. This is often the case with religious novels since fiction is riskier (from the publisher's view) than nonfiction.

If or when you send a complete manuscript, you may be in for a very long wait before you get a final decision. Unless you have the time to write a full manuscript (without a commitment) and wait several more months to get a decision on it, I advise you to deal only with those religious publishers who are willing to reach a decision on an outline and a chapter or two.

7. Consider this idea: If your religious-inspirational book is a title that could cross borders and sell in both secular and religious markets, you might try to place the book with a general publisher that also includes religious-inspirational titles in its list of books.

More and more, religious publishers are selling their books in Christian bookstores as well as general bookstores. General publishers are doing the same thing, trying to get more of their suitable books into Christian bookstores. The point is that your book will sell more copies if it can be on the shelves of *both* religious and general bookstores.

A Quick Warning

I don't know why, but some religious book publishers just aren't as professional, courteous, and businesslike as many general publishers are. Maybe it's because they are smaller companies. Some religious publishers do not offer an advance against royalties. If you do business with such a company, you must realize that it may be some time before the book is published and on sale. Some publishers can get a book on the market in six months. Others take a year or even longer.

Rewards of Writing Religious-Inspirational Books

Despite some of the disadvantages of writing this kind of book, there are definite rewards to be gained. The advantages include the following:

- The satisfaction of knowing that your book may help someone at a crucial period in his or her life.
- The great variety of inspirational and religious subjects that you may choose.
- The joy of seeing your book sell in Christian and secular (general) bookstores.
- A chance to share your personal experience with readers and to tell what your own faith has meant to you.
- The opportunity to lead others closer to God.
- The satisfaction of knowing that your book may be around for many years to come and even go on helping readers after you're gone. Some of these books can last for a generation or longer.

18
Business and Professional Books

Business books are always of interest to publishers and book buyers as well. Even in bad economic periods (or great ones), business books continue to move out of the stores. Many years ago, I remember having to search for various business books near the back of the stores. Sometimes they were tucked away in the far right- or left-hand corner of the store. It's just the opposite today.

Business books are now "up front" in a number of ways. The entire business section is almost next to the checkout counter in many bookstores. Selected business books are on featured display where customers see them as soon as they walk into a lot of stores. Many stores include sections specifically categorized under Investing, Small Business, Careers, or Management. Some stores have entire sections on the stock market. Lots of these sections are smack-dab in the front of the store, even if they may be against the wall.

Computer books are usually placed very close to the business section, if not actually in it. This way, customers are led easily and naturally from the business to the computer section or vice-versa. There is often an entire technical section of books.

The point is that business books have "arrived." They have come into their own and are in demand. I predict that business books will continue to sell well and maintain their popular momentum in the coming decades. One of my mega-star selling books, one I did back in the 1980s, was a business book. I must quickly add that the book got all the right breaks via a terrific cover design, ongoing strong promotion, and lots of publicity, book club interest, and the rest.

Bookstores around the country realized the importance of business books with the arrival of the high-tech era, the demand for computer books, software, and other similar products. All these influences acted together like a super tonic for the business book category. The result is that business books, in all their forms, continue to sell, and at times, certain ones can even blast their way up the sales charts.

This kind of book can go on selling for many years. Here are some examples:
- *The One Minute Manager*
- *Crisis Management*
- *The Banking Jungle*
- *The Official Stockbroker's Handbook*
- *A Guide to Controlling Your Corporation's Future*
- *Money Dynamics* (this one came out in new editions for different years.)
- *Maverick Career Strategies*
- *Successful Time Management*
- *Money in Your Mailbox* (This was the mega-star seller yours truly did.)

Should You Do a Business Book?

Perhaps you should decide now to write a business book. If you have given some thought about what your next (or even your first) book should be, I want to recommend trying your hand at a business book. Here are just a few sound reasons why you would be wise to choose this type of book:

- Business books sell better than other, more general, categories of trade books.
- Business books can keep paying royalties for their authors for years. The first one I did stayed in print for close to 10 years. Others I did went on even longer.
- Many editors are interested in acquiring new business books. If your book gets turned down by a few editors, there are others you can try.
- You may now have first-hand business knowledge that you could put to work in a book. You may even be in a business category now via your job and could spin off a book about it. Being on the inside, you already know a lot about it.
- Various foreign publishers are often interested in the rights to business books published in America, since the same information can benefit readers overseas.

Big Business Book Examples

Remember the book *Megatrends*? It was a blockbuster, a super-business book that took America by storm. It was featured in all major media and made a fortune for its author. *Megatrends* was followed by *Reinventing the Corporation* by the same author, John Naisbitt. The business book category has treated him handsomely. It could do the same for you, if you have something important, helpful, or well-worth saying and can communicate it effectively in writing.

Another big book was *In Search of Excellence*, which was enormously popular from coast to coast, overseas, and just about everywhere. It doesn't take a crystal ball to know that other business books to be published in future years will be very successful. To get in on the action, start planning and writing your own business book. This type of book is a winner with the book-buying public, no matter what the current times or era may happen to be. The business book will always be a popular mainstay in this industry.

How to Plan and Write a Business Book

Here is a series of steps to follow that will help you get started on writing a business book manuscript. Most of these are the exact steps I followed in selling a number of business books to major publishers:

1. Decide on the business subject of your choice. If you're already at work in the daily business world, there are book ideas all around you, but you have to be able to recognize them. Watch for ideas in business reports you may read or see, during speeches you hear, business conferences and seminars you attend, and even in the conversations with business associates and friends. Ideas are there, so be alert for them.

By way of example, a brochure advertising a seminar crossed my desk just today. A casual glance at this brochure suggested six possible new business books. Here are a few of them just as they hit me:

- *Speed Reading for Managers*
- *How to Delegate Effectively*
- *The Key to Gaining Management Time*

2. Research the subject of your choice, and this means reading articles, books, reports, special studies, attending lectures if possible, interviewing known authorities, and finding any and all pertinent information possible.

3. With a quantity of relevant material narrowed down to the most pertinent at the ready, write an outline listing the heading of each chapter for your table of contents.

4. Using the outline as a guide, start chapter one, striving to grab reader interest and hold it throughout. The first chapter is

very important in hooking the reader. The first few *pages* of your book are critical because often the reader will decide only after reading them whether to buy your book or not.

5. Complete the rest of the chapters for your book. Then go back over the entire manuscript making corrections, additions, and cuts where needed, and rewriting.

6. Decide whether to do another rewrite or type it clean after you feel you cannot improve it any more.

7. Once it is neatly typed, you're ready to contact a publisher (preferably a specific editor at the company), and ask if the editor would be interested. Try to send your e-mail (or snail mail letter) to an editor at that publishing company who seems to manage similar books. Do not send your letter (or book) to publishers who are not doing the type of book you're offering. Why reduce the odds that way? Match your book project to publishers and editors who actually publish similar books.

One helpful way to find your right subject is to list the businesses or industries you've had experience in over the years. Perhaps you have some particular or special knowledge or information about advertising, insurance, safety and security, the stock market, futures, other investing, management, banking, transportation, music (as a business), real estate, lumber, beauty secrets, or other business type subjects.

It's possible that you already have enough knowledge of a particular business or profession to make at least a good start on a book. Search your own background and experience for clues.

A Practical Idea

Any number of companies would like to have books written about them, but they don't have the time or help for such a project. A number of managers, for example, have admitted the need for books about their organizations. Some are actively looking for authors to write such books. I believe this is an untapped market for possible new book sales for authors everywhere. Naturally, the company brass must be interested in such a project.

Whether you try to place a book project with a recognized publisher or with a business corporation, you will find some of the following directories and source books very useful. They can usually be found in large libraries. Here are just a few:
- *National Directory of Associations*
- *National Directory of Public Relations Directors*
- *Gale's Encyclopedia of Associations*
- *Public Relations Register*
- *MacRae's Blue Book (Index of Companies)*
- *Thomas Register of American Manufacturers*

Don't forget to use the ever-increasing resources and information galore found on the internet. Never forget in your writing future the vast and important research tool you have sitting on your desk via your own computer. It's a great advantage over the authors of earlier decades.

Computer Books

Adjacent to or very near the business section you will usually find other sections in bookstores marked Computer Books.

It's a well-known fact in the industry that most of the leading publishers went overboard on computer books in their earlier years. Despite the excitement and high-profit stories that circulated with the arrival of America's high-tech era, the market was only able to absorb a certain number of computer books and software products. During this time, leading publishers simply produced far too many computer books, and the market was glutted with them, like it sometimes is with romance novels. More and more publishers jumped aboard the computer bandwagon until, finally, a number of them lost a lot of money. They finally realized they had overproduced. Keep this fact in mind that even publishers can and do make mistakes, just as authors sometimes do. I'm sure most publishers are wiser for the experience.

There you have it. When you sit down to think about what your very first book, or the twentieth, will be, give some real thought to doing a business book. I have a special "thank you" place in my mind, heart, and spirit for the business book, which was the category that did best (so far) for me in my own writing career. I now have books in other categories, including the novel, that may eventually do even better than my business books.

Consider all possible categories and the descriptions given in this book. Then make your decision. Imagine all the people out there – in the business arena, the potential book buyers – that can be helped, led, informed, and inspired by your business book. I wish you well in this always interesting category. Your very first business book may change a lot of lives. So think B for business – a business book you created.

19
Textbooks Can Work for You

❖ ❖ ❖

Many authors are not interested in writing textbooks. They're more interested in a standard nonfiction book or novel. There are indeed writers who cringe at the thought of doing a textbook. "All that technical and detailed work would get on my nerves," they say. Or "I would rather write mass-market paperbacks, children's books, or general nonfiction trade books."

No book about authorship is complete, however, without citing the case for writing textbooks. A successful textbook could finance your writing career for years to come. Just one successful textbook used by the junior college market can bring upwards of 30 thousand dollars a year or more for its author, though some textbooks are done by two or more authors. The amount such books can earn depend on how much they sell for and how well they do in the marketplace. Some authors with textbook sales call them "golden annuities."

Textbooks are definitely worth the time and effort necessary to write and sell them. Or should I say sell and write them?

Remember, the smart author sells first and *then* completes the manuscript. Textbooks also don't have to be a mass of technical and complicated details. The emphasis now is on those that communicate in a less technical way. Naturally, some subjects are much more technical and involved.

The trick to striking it rich – or close – with a textbook is to write one that is adopted by community colleges and regular four-year universities everywhere. Textbooks that catch on can be used for many years. If they do become definitive works in their respective subject areas, their authors are going to make a lot of money. One highly acclaimed author wrote a math textbook a number of years back. He has reportedly made well over a million dollars so far from this *one* book.

Royalties for Textbooks

Textbook royalties range from 8 to 15 percent of the *net* price received by the publisher. Authors' royalties for textbooks are based on the net revenue received by the publisher for the specific book because schools and colleges order at bulk prices. Some textbook authors get better royalty deals, though, while the royalties are smaller for an elementary or high school textbook. Some writers with a good track record, however, may succeed in obtaining higher royalty rates even for these. I've heard reports of some textbook authors getting a 20 percent royalty rate.

You may be able to write a textbook for any of the following markets:
- Elementary schools
- High schools
- Community colleges
- Four-year universities
- Graduate schools
- Trade schools
- Continuing adult education

If you have done any teaching, you may find it easier to complete a textbook. The subject you taught would be a natural possibility for you. I've taught journalism, creative writing, English, speech, literature, composition, and other courses on both the secondary and university levels. I have also taught for the United States Navy aboard certain ships and at naval bases. As yet, I have not tried my hand at writing a textbook on any of these subjects, but I may well write one in the future.

In other words, teaching experience is a definite advantage. After all, a teacher already knows a great deal about the chosen subject. Another way to find a possible textbook subject is to search your memory. Think back on your school days. Which subjects did you enjoy the most? Write them down and decide on the one you like best. Then make a start.

Again, the best time to sell a textbook is before you are well into the book. Do an outline of what you would cover. Then try to interest a suitable textbook publisher. Keep in mind that many textbooks are longer than general trade books and often run several hundred to four hundred pages or more.

You will probably have to write one or more chapters of your textbook at least before trying to sell your book. And you will need a good outline that shows your plan for the book. The kind of money you can potentially make from textbooks is worth the investment of time and effort. It is certainly worth trying in between some other book projects. Just realize at the start that writing a textbook will take a considerably longer time in most cases.

What Teachers Want

According to recent surveys in education magazines, the majority of elementary teachers believe there should be more emphasis on reading and writing skills. In their opinion, a new focus on these skills would improve student achievement. Of 8,500 teachers polled, just over 41 percent strongly agreed on the need for better textbooks.

Education needs and wants better and more useful textbooks that are meant for the students of today. Write a better one that does the job more effectively for students, and you might well have a winner.

More Cooperation Between Stores and Publishers

One big change in the textbook business today is the increased harmony between publishers and store managers (at the time of this writing). As one college store association executive put it, "There's a much more professional relationship between college publishers and the store managers than in a number of years."

Why Not Try A Textbook?

All you current authors out there, the going-to-be authors, and the want-to-be authors should ask yourselves this question. Why try a textbook? Well, why not then? All you have to lose is some time and effort in trying to discover if you might be interested in writing a textbook.

Explore the subjects of interest to you, any you may have taught or know a lot about, and talk to some college professors plus teachers about their future textbook needs. It would be a great idea to actually visit some college bookstores to see the published texts now being used by students. Some authors like this book category so much that they prefer to specialize in it. You will never know if there's a textbook in you until you explore the idea.

If you do go ahead with this book category, and if one or more of your textbooks gets adopted by various schools, you may well be sitting pretty, meaning your royalty checks will be much higher. More text power to you.

20
Don't Forget Humor Books!

"The world is forty laughs behind," said the immortal actor Humphrey Bogart. Since laughter and humor are part and parcel of what makes life worth living, you should give some thought to the idea of writing a humorous book.

Some memorable humor books that sold big include *The Official Preppy Handbook*, all of Art Buchwald's books and more or less all of the other popular humorists' works of past and present.

One curious example was *The Nothing Book*, which was a great example of the nonbook. It was a mind-boggling success with over a million copies sold. It's jolting when you consider that there was nothing in the book between the covers but blank pages. Kind of reminds me of the pet rock success. *The Nothing Book* went on selling for years.

Examples of Humor Books
- *Be Careful, in College I Used to Box a Little*
- *How to Be an Italian*
- *Zombie Jamboree*

- *English Well Speeched Here (and Other Fractured Expressions from Around the World)*
- *No Laughing Matter*
- *Fatherhood Is Not Pretty*
- *If the Boss Calls, I'm in a Sails Meeting (Confessions of a Boataholic)*

You need to be aware of some realities about the humor and the nonbook. Generally speaking, humor books are considered hard to write. But if you have a natural gift for humor, for making people laugh or feel amused, you might do a fine book. The odds are strongly against you without some degree of talent for humor. Persons who can write humor and come up with offbeat, unique ideas for nonbooks usually know it. Some of the highest paid people in television are comedy writers. The big name comedians pay their staff writers excellent money to think up those clever lines and funny situations.

If you have a burning desire to write a humor book, or collection of funny, witty material, go to it. You might just pull it off and come up with a winner. The point I want you to remember via this chapter is not to forget or ignore this book category. A humor book may be the last type you would want to write at this time, but who knows – next year or five years from now you may change your mind.

Ideas for Humor Books

Ideas for this book category may come from anywhere, but here are some sources to be aware of on a regular basis:
- Chance remarks you overhear almost anywhere.
- All the media (newspapers, books, comic strips, magazines, television, radio, and the big screen).
- Joke books of all kinds.
- Thinking back on funny things that have happened to you, your family members, relatives, and friends.

- Think about humor in general and what is funny or amusing.
- Frequently read the punch lines on studio and humorous greeting cards in stores.
- Look at humor sources including satire, sarcasm, irony, plays on words, parody, associations, and burlesque.

What Is Humor?

Here is a good definition of humor: "A comic quality causing amusement: the humor of a situation." It's also been defined as "the faculty of perceiving what is amusing or comical."

To take something known and familiar and then make it seem funny is an art. Useful tools to help you accomplish it are:
- Association
- Understatement
- Surprise (A lot of humor uses the element of surprise.)
- Exaggeration

One of the strongest examples of situation humor was a film some years back (now a classic humor movie) called *The Out-of-Towners*. It starred Jack Lemmon and Sandy Dennis. Every conceivable thing went wrong on this Ohio couple's trip to New York. The reactions of the characters – especially Jack Lemmon – were hilarious. After a number of bad events happened to them, it became funny to watch Lemmon's reactions, such as his writing the hotel desk clerk's name down and threatening to sue the hotel over and over for giving their reservations away.

Some publishers are always looking for authors who have a talent for writing funny books. If you can deliver the goods, you could have a very successful book in this category and maybe a bestseller. Remember, however, that it has to be good. Some writers with a gift for humor specialize in this type of book. Certainly all such books do a lot to help readers enjoy their daily lives.

If you can do it, make them laugh. Then *you* get to laugh – all the way to the bank. I hope one or more of the top humor books of the future might have your name on the covers. It's a worthy and challenging book category.

Some Publishers That Like Humor Books

- Piccadilly Books (Colorado Springs)
- Workman Publishing Company (New York)
- Price/Stern/Sloan Publishers (Los Angeles)
- Peachtree Publishers (Atlanta)

So if and when you go for a humor book, enjoy yourself. Get yourself in a funny, laughing mood, for that may well trigger it for the author you are or hope to be. Decades later now, I still remember Donald O'Connor, the very talented dancer-actor, in a hilarious dance scene titled "Make 'Em Laugh." It wasn't a book, but the humor quality was absolutely astounding. Keep in mind that the humor book you may well write one day could upgrade the lives of a lot of readers out there. It's a lot easier of course to show humor on the big screen, in a funny musical dance sequence, than to get sparkling humor to leap out at the reader from the words and pages of a book.

Good luck and make 'em laugh. The whole world is forty laughs behind.

21
Mass-Market Paperback Originals

Perhaps the biggest bucks an author can ever hope to make lie in mass-market paperbacks. This might be the kind of writing for you. Paul Little, a prolific author, first entered the paperback field many years ago. In just two years, he had 26 books published.

Paperbacks cover a variety of subjects. Even the joys of reading have been written about in a paperback – *The New Hooked on Books*, which went through many editions.

One paperback, *When Bad Things Happen to Good People*, has gone back to press more than 21 times and has some two million copies in print. Author Cynthia Freeman started writing years ago after giving up a career in interior design because of illness. Her very first novel, *A World Full of Strangers*, sold over two million copies in paperback. She found herself an overnight celebrity.

The Test of a Mass-Market Paperback Idea

Whenever you think you may have a hot idea for a mass-market paperback, check it out with the following questions:

1. Would enough people be interested in the book? Mass market means appeal for millions of readers.

2. Do I have enough interest in the idea to see it through to completion? You would be surprised how many manuscripts are started but never finished.

3. Is the idea commercial enough for the leading paperback publisher?

Getting the Feel for Mass-Market Paperbacks

As you might expect, the best way to develop a feel for this kind of book is to read the novels of Tom Clancy, Clive Cussler, Rosemary Rogers, Peter Benchley (author of *Jaws*), Harold Robbins, Jackie Collins, and other authors who have emerged in the field during recent years.

These authors, and others you can name yourself, have enormous appeal for the masses. Their books are filled with excitement, adventure, mystery, and glamour – all the ingredients that millions of readers cannot resist. The books offer plenty of escape from the burdens, boredom, and disappointments of modern life. Read *Don't Sweat the Small Stuff*, which quickly became a national bestseller and on-going classic that readers everywhere responded to with gusto and relish.

Mass-market paperbacks can be adventure novels, spy capers, romance novels, suspense thrillers like *Eye of the Needle*, horror stories, or love stories. They have plenty of action and entertain the reader in a number of ways.

The Amazing Harold Robbins

Though he's been gone now for some years, Robbins is a good example of how far an author can go in the paperback field. He called himself "the people's writer." His book sales proved it. Some of his early books, like *The Adventurers* and *The Carpetbaggers*, sold 10 million copies or more every year.

Robbins became an expert at blending sin and sex into his novels. His characters were often beautiful people caught up in compelling situations. Robbins grew up in the Hell's Kitchen area of New York but became a multi-millionaire via his books. When he was working on a book, he isolated himself and kept the curtains down on the windows. He often used a drab hotel room to do his writing. This isolation method evidently worked well for him.

Mario Puzo: Paperback Godfather

Time magazine deemed Mario Puzo the "paperback Godfather." The reprint rights for *Fools Die* were sold for an enormous sum for that time. The book was on the bestseller lists long before its publication date.

You don't have to read far in Puzo's books to realize his outstanding descriptive abilities. He makes you see what's happening just as though it were taking place on a stage before your eyes.

The story goes that Puzo wrote most of *The Godfather* on the kitchen table of his New York home. After the book became an international success, and Puzo had access to a fancy office and desk, he couldn't write a word. He had to go back to his kitchen table. This is true for a number of authors. If you find a place – wherever it is – that works well for you, stick with it and write your books there.

Puzo is gone now too, but he will live on in the pages of his highly successful and well done novels. He was also one of the story-screenplay writers for the first *Superman* film, considered by a great many to be the best of the franchise.

Clive Cussler: An Author Who Lives His Adventures

Multi-millionaire author Clive Cussler is a friend of mine, and I once ate lunch with him at a Colorado State University conference where he was the main speaker. He worked in advertising for years before turning to books, and to this day Clive still collects old vintage cars. He has a home out from Denver and another one in Arizona.

One of the nicest and most professional authors I have ever met or known, Clive Cussler's first big bestseller was *Raise the Titanic*. Since then, he has written a number of other bestsellers like *Sahara, Deep Six, Cyclops,* and others.

Clive's lead character in his exciting novels is Dirk Pitt, who gets involved in challenging missions on the high seas of world intrigue. The first thing I realized about Clive after meeting and talking with him is what a truly masterful storyteller he is. For novels, that is the most important skill you can have. He simply tells a fascinating story.

Clive Cussler is much like his lead character, Dirk Pitt. He's an adventurer in the sense that he enjoys searching for old ships that went down hundreds of years ago. When not working on a new novel, Cussler and his crew are off to some locale in the world on a search for a new sunken ship. He is credited with having located the German U-boat that sank the *Lusitania*. They located the exact spot where the German U-boat lies beneath the sea. Cussler passed along that information to officials so that a record now exists of where the German submarine lies.

In writing novels, Cussler believes that a novelist should make every effort to end each chapter with a hook so that the reader thinks, "My God, what happens next?" This keeps the reader turning pages.

Here are some other very helpful, valid guidelines for writing fiction from Clive Cussler:
- The ending is absolutely vital. "Readers want the good guys to win and the villains to lose."
- "If you're really a book writer, before you finish one book, you've got an idea for the next one." I can vouch for this fact. It's always been the case for me.
- "A novelist is an inventor creating a product. If the product is not good, you aren't going to sell it."

- "I always send in the finished product [manuscript]. I prefer to do it this way."
- "Try and resolve a problem in a book before you go on to another one."
- "I write one page at a time. I edit a chapter on the screen till it's ready. I go back and change a few sentences and add something."
- "When I type the end, I'm usually through. I may go back and do a little rewriting." (Cussler gets all the work done on each chapter before moving on to the next one. So when he reaches the end of the novel, he's usually through except for some final rewriting on occasion.)
- "A good editor or agent will read the first paragraph and if it doesn't take off, forget it."
- "I try to write a fast-paced book. The meat of the story is dialogue. The heavier the dialogue, the faster the pace."
- "When I'm working on a book, I never read."
- "An author should get an office and write all day. There are too many interruptions at home."

Clive Cussler's willingness to give his advice, and tell how he does it, has been an inspiration to many other authors for years. It was a genuine pleasure to meet him. I also heard him speak at another meeting a few years earlier in Norman, Oklahoma, and once again he went out of his way to encourage other authors and share his valued views about the business. What he has said has been of enormous help to me in my own writing, and it may aid you as well.

There's an old adage in publishing and writing in general that "writers are insanely jealous of each other." In some cases, it is quite true, but in the case of the talented Clive Cussler, you would never know what enormous success he has achieved in novel writing merely by speaking with him. Quite simply, he is like your next-door neighbor – just a regular fellow who happens to have developed a stunning talent for writing adventure novels.

22
Ghostwriting Has a New Name

The new name for ghostwriting is "collaborative writing." When an expert wants to write a book, but is not very good at the actual writing process, he or she will often use the services of a professional author. If the pro author's name does not appear on the cover, then the book has been ghostwritten. If the expert doing the book decides to share the credit with the writer, then the author's name will also appear on the book usually in one of three ways: "As told to," "and," or "with," followed by the pro author's name.

As you have no doubt seen in many bookstores, most well-known celebrities from the entertainment industry, broadcasting, politics, the government, and business world are unable to write their own books without help (with some exceptions). So they work with a professional author. The resulting title covers read "as told to William Novak," or "with Kitty Kelly."

The point is that the authors who choose to collaborate must work out an arrangement with the expert or celebrity. There should be a *written agreement* on how the writer is to be compensated for his work on the book.

A good example of collaborative writing is the Lee Iacocca book. William Novak was a Boston author with three nonfiction books to his credit, but he had reached the conclusion that it was next to impossible for an author to make a living, at least at that time period. Then, out of the blue, an editor friend in New York called and asked if Novak would be interested in collaborating with Iacocca on his memoirs. Novak accepted, and the result was a blockbuster book that sold a huge 2.5 million copies. And the book just kept on selling for years.

There was a time, not very long ago, when the celebrity's name alone appeared on the book. Any professional who helped write the book – part or all of it – had to be content with the money he received as the "ghost." It's a different story today. Collaborative authors have come into their own. Major book projects now offer collaborative authors the chance to pull down substantial sums of money.

Until now, ghostwriters were usually paid a flat fee varying from 10,000 to 100,000 dollars per book. Since coming into their own, collaborative authors can now receive *half* of a bestselling book's earnings. So, in effect, the doors have swung wide open today for authors who collaborate with well-known people. A lot of money can be at stake if and when the resulting books achieve bestseller status. The better the celebrity is known, the higher the chances for success.

There's another change, too, that has taken place for collaborative authors. In the words of one Random House publishing executive, "Their work is not only more glamorous because of the success of collaborations like *Iacocca* and *Yeager*. It's regarded now less as tradesman's work than many people realize. It takes great skill, and a lot of self-effacing grace." What has happened is that ghostwriters have become collaborative authors and now receive cover line credit for their work.

A key reason such writers are in demand is simply because more books of memoirs are being written today. More celebrities from different fields are choosing to write books, so they need the help and skills of a collaborative writer. The huge success of some of these books has opened the door to collaborative authors.

What Constitutes Collaborative Writing?

When a professional author agrees to collaborate with a celebrity on a book, a commitment is made to do the following:
- Work out a plan and structure for the book.
- Ask probing questions that will bring the best responses from the celebrity. This helps to focus on choice material.
- Steer the work in progress and strive to write a quality book.

When a celebrity, or public figure, decides to do a book, a literary agency or publisher is contacted. Then the agent or publishing house looks for the right author to work with the celebrity. There must be rapport between the two, if the resulting book is to be an effective one. According to one editor at a major New York publishing house, "Finding the right author is vital. It can spell the difference between a pretty good book and an excellent one."

William Novak was offered a flat fee for his work on *Iacocca*. He chose to accept the fee, reported to be 45,000 dollars plus a 35,000 dollar bonus. This was a good deal at that time. Remember, the book came out some years back. Nobody knew in the beginning what a huge success the resulting book would turn out to be. Novak now has a share in the royalties on celebrity books he agrees to collaborate on and write.

Samm Sinclair Baker, who has done collaborative work (with Irwin Stillman on *The Doctor's Quick Weight Loss Diet*), believes the arrangement between celebrity and author should be equal: "No partnership is any good that isn't fifty-fifty. Otherwise, the expert is saying the author is inferior." Baker insists on a fifty-fifty royalty split plus an "and" credit.

Keep this type of collaborative writing in mind. Tell editors you know, or work with in the future, of your interest in collaborative work with celebrities and public figures. If you sign with an agent for representation, let him or her know that you would be happy to consider any collaborative writing deals.

All in all, this type of work has opened up an exciting option for today's authors. Keep up with collaborative writing in the future. It might just give your writing career a boost that could land you on the bestseller lists and keep your bank account smiling.

23
Promotional Opportunities

❖ ❖ ❖

In this chapter, I will discuss the promotion of your books. As mentioned earlier, some authors forget a book once it has been published. They're usually involved in a new project by then.

There are two types of promotion: what your publisher can do for the book and what you can accomplish yourself. Anything you can do for each of your books will help of course, so keep this in mind.

There are positive things you can do to promote your book. If you can't drive across the nation seeing bookstore managers about your book, you can take other steps. To refresh your memory and give you a workable promotion plan, refer back to this chapter each time one of your books is published. Here is the plan:

1. Make the rounds of all the bookstores in your city, town, or community area. Tell them about your book and try to arrange an autograph session in some of the major stores. Many bookstore owners and managers are receptive to having authors appear in their stores. Such appearances sell books.

2. Do anything and everything you can to get on local radio and television programs. You can e-mail or write the station or specific talk show personality or go to the station in person. You will probably have to make an appointment to see the Program Manager, Public Relations Director, or other appropriate person.

3. Tell everyone possible about your book and send e-mails or write letters about it to all your friends and relatives. You can easily phone all your friends and relatives about your book without it taking too much time.

4. Try to interest local and regional newspaper writers in doing a feature article about you and your new book. Most city papers have a book review or literary page. Call or write newspapers of your choice and ask whom you should contact. Try to get a personal meeting with the right editor, columnist, or staff writer. You may well *not* get replies to your e-mails or snail mail letters, so go to these newspapers in person if at all possible. That will improve your chances of getting some attention.

5. Contact any and all related trade journals and publications about your book. If your book is on pet care, for example, the leading magazines in the pet industry should be contacted. If your book covers a business subject, there are numerous publications to consider. See the current editions of *Writer's Market* and the magazine section of *Literary Market Place*.

6. Consider the idea of writing a feature article about your book yourself. It's possible that a national, regional, or local magazine or newspaper might use it. If your book is timely, chances are even better that your feature article will be used.

7. Watch the book trade publications like *Publisher's Weekly* and *Writer's Journal* for leads on book reviewers. The circulations of various newspapers and magazines are large.

8. Quite a few daily newspapers have a Sunday magazine section. E-mail, call, or write to the managing editor of each about your book. I would include in your list *The Chicago Tribune, Family Weekly, The New York Times Magazine, Columbus Dispatch,*

Seattle Times and don't forget to check your own area's Sunday magazine section.

9. Look for some angle that a magazine or newspaper editor could use to publicize your book. For example, will it help readers save money, learn the truth about something, make more money, get a job, or advance in their present position? The following people could be helpful in promoting your book:
- Booksellers
- Librarians
- Advertising agencies and ad copywriters
- Book reviewers
- Book salespeople
- Book sales teams
- Columnists
- Fraternal club officers
- Civic club leaders
- Radio and television producers plus talk-show personalities
- Editors of magazines, newspapers, trade journals, newsletters, and bulletins plus fraternity-sorority magazines.
- Public-Relations directors
- Club women
- Historical societies
- All kinds of special clubs and hobby groups
- National and international association directors
- Book club officials
- A variety of government agencies
- Religious organizations, if your book is a religious one or would interest them

10. Write a direct sales letter in which you tell about yourself and your book. Send the e-mail or snail mail letter to a list of radio and television program directors, producers, and talk-show personalities who may be receptive to having you as a guest author.

Send your sales letter to a wide variety of stations. In fact, go ahead and send your sales letter to anyone you think might help promote your book. With e-mail communication, you can reach a lot of people very easily.

11. Consider "self-syndicating" a feature article or review about your book. You can get the names of many newspaper editors in yearly directories published by *Editor and Publisher*.

Publicity Stunts

Sometimes clever and unusual publicity stunts can send the sales of a book skyrocketing. If you're an imaginative and somewhat daring author, you might consider dreaming up some kind of publicity stunt to attract attention to your book. With so many thousands of new books coming out each year, the more attention you can get for your book the better chance it will have to break out and go somewhere.

A man who ran for governor of Tennessee once walked across his entire state to get attention for his book. He received regular publicity for the walk and was shown talking to people all along the way. Stories about him were featured on many evening news programs.

He made a mark on his map at the end of each day to show where he had stopped, then resumed his walk at his marker the next morning. It was an effective idea and worked well for him. There may be one or more clues in your book for a possible publicity stunt you could do. The questions to ask yourself include the following:
- What could I [you] do to attract favorable attention and publicity for my book?
- Are there any unusual ways to advertise my book?
- Could I arrange to get any local, regional, or national celebrity to plug my book?

- Could I do something dramatic that might increase the sales of my book, like bicycle across the nation or rent a billboard sign with an unusual message on it?
- Is there anything unique, shocking, timely, or newsworthy about the book that might get me an interview-guest appearance on "Good Morning, America," "Today," "The Tonight Show," or any of the lesser known, regional, or even local radio-television programs? Naturally, top shows like "Good Morning, America," and others can do wonders for the sales of a book. Just keep in mind that the competition is enormous. Find out who interviews authors for possible bookings on these shows. Call them up, e-mail them, and write snail mail letters too. Be persistent. You might just land something. This is the very way I got myself on a number of regional radio and television talk shows and news programs. It works, but it takes time and persistence.

Get in Touch With Newspaper Columnists

There are columns written on all kinds of subjects. Your book may be of interest to the readers of columns on lifestyles, business, money matters, the arts, self-help subjects, religion, marriage, or whatever. The circulation of many columns runs in the hundreds of thousands or millions. A mention of your book by the columnist could be a real promotional shot in the arm for it. According to reports, a favorable mention of a book in certain columns has brought amazing sales results. See the current *Literary Market Place* (a key directory you should have and use) for addresses of columnists.

One final bit of advice is this: You must keep in mind that newspapers (at this writing) are dying. When bad economic eras hit, newspapers can suffer, but the decline is also due to the rise of computers and the internet. Millions today get all the latest news right on their computers. This is hurting newspapers big time, just like the rise of e-mail use has cut down post office profits.

Good luck with the promotion you do for each of your books. If you have your own website or blog, they are both naturals to promote your books and sell them. Publishers expect you to do effective promotion. It can only help each of your books and give you the opportunity to get on eventually with the next book. Never give up promoting any book of yours that you believe in and know will help or entertain readers out there everywhere. Promote with enthusiasm and vitality. You'll be glad you did.

24
The Truth About Self-Publishing

If you cannot find a publisher worthy to handle your book, take another route before scrapping your project. You can publish your book yourself. Today there are even online companies that will help you get your book into print, but I advise you to check them out carefully before going ahead with it.

I still think it's better to find a traditional book publisher than going the do-it-yourself route. There are some unusual accounts of self-publishers who have made fortunes by doing everything themselves, but most authors out there choose the traditional route, which means that the publisher they sign with does the book.

I don't advise self-publishing for most authors unless all or the majority of the following factors are true in your case:
- You've tried 30 or more recognized legitimate book publishers, and all of them have rejected your book. Many authors try 50 (or more) before they give up and try another creation. Some authors never give up. They just start a new round of submissions and often sell via the second campaign.

- You're hell-bent on seeing your book published, no matter what.
- You have the money necessary to finance the publication of your own book, plus some necessary promotion for it.
- You have a very strong belief that your book will sell, backed up with research or data or preliminary marketing indications.
- You have a nagging feeling that you should publish the book and the feeling persists over a period of time.
- You're willing to do everything possible to promote your book after you publish it. This means trying to line up radio-television interviews, publicity, in-store promotion, featuring the book on your own website, blog, or wherever else you can spotlight it.

Remember, in today's publishing arena, some large New York publishers won't even consider an author's new book unless that person can assure the publisher of a "platform" or ways to sell it (via the author's own website, speaking programs, seminars, and so on). In other words, some of the major publishers expect the author of today to do much more than turn out a masterpiece. Before even daring to approach certain publishers, editors, or star agents, some of these companies almost demand that the author prove upfront that the book will be a national, preferably worldwide, bestseller. This is apparently the case for a small number of big-city publishers. Most publishers still treat authors in a professional manner, but if you deal or communicate with the "big boys" (as some authors call them), I'm simply warning you to be prepared.

I'm afraid the years and era are gone when publishing was referred to as the "gentleman's business." I'm talking about that great era when legendary editor Max Perkins was alive, well, and working with Fitzgerald, Thomas Wolfe, and Hemingway. Editors had much more power then and did not "fall at the feet" of powerhouse agents. Big-name agents have taken much of the power once held by editors away. Agents today are considered the gatekeepers of the business, and some of them guard it like they're playing a game of capture the flag. Any would-be author trying to get by them had better exceed excellence or be booted back into the briar patch.

What I'm relating here is based on a number of decades (I won't say how many!) in the business and active participation in all phases of it. I'm hopeful, and at least expect, *new authors* to read this book (as well as veteran authors). By far, most publishers, editors, and agents treat authors well, work with them professionally, and are caring, kind, and courteous. I do not want new authors who read this book to be discouraged when and *if* they encounter some of the publishing industry's less shining individuals. My advice to all authors (new and veteran) is to simply roll with the blow and *get on with your writing career*.

The Concept of Self-Publishing

The self-publishing view is that just about anyone with a strong book idea can publish the manuscript, provided there is money available. There are thousands of very small author-publisher firms, many of them in California but also other states and countries. The authors' market directories even sometimes include a "Small Press" section. If the books of some of these small publishers take off in the marketplace, these self-publishers can do very well. They get to keep the lion's share of the profits their books earn, too. They don't have to split with a traditional publisher. Even in a standard contract between an author and major publisher, the author is low man (or woman) on the totem pole. The publisher makes the most with the author getting a royalty percentage. Online, electronic publishers are growing, however, and offering a new way to go for authors. Self-publishers can now also sell their books via the internet and make sales worldwide.

For some authors, self-publishing may be easier than dealing with a traditional company. Some authors want, and seem to enjoy, doing it all – writing, producing, printing, selling, and promoting the book. You can be sure, too, that self-publishers will not let their new books "die on the vine," as some large national book publishers do using the "shotgun approach" and just throwing a lot of new books into the marketplace.

Every book is a lead book for a self-publisher, who sinks a lot of time, money, effort, and sacrifice into one or more given books. If their gamble pays off, the self-publisher makes a bundle. The books of some self-publishers can sometimes do far better than many of the carloads of new books issued by large mainline publishers.

Sales of a book in the first year are critical and usually determine what its fate will be, when controlled by a large national publisher. It may die a quick death by or before the end of the first year. The self-publisher acts differently. The first year is used to build a solid market for a future of sustained sales. A big New York publisher may sell only five thousand copies total, but the self-publisher can usually count on five thousand copies or more each year. The books of self-publishers can go on selling for decades instead of being "dead in the water" after a year or two.

You should realize that a self-published book often has a better chance of success because it's under the control of one who cares – the author. Dan Poynter, a self-publisher when he began, sold 125,000 copies of a book on a new sport. It reportedly took him two months of writing time. One can only wonder what sales of the book would have been if it had been published by a large national company; my guess is that they would have been only a fraction of Poynter's self-published total.

A successful woman lawyer in the Midwest once finished a first novel and sent it off to a likely publisher. After six months of waiting, her manuscript was finally returned. Undaunted, she sent it off to another traditional publisher. After over a *year and a half* passed, she finally received another rejection. So what did she do? She published her book herself, doing the artwork and handling its printing and distribution. Her book started selling and soon attracted a west coast agent, who signed the self-published author-lawyer as a client. Her literary agent sold the paperback rights for a reported million dollars. This can happen. My point is that lightning can strike for a self-publisher. And the self-publisher keeps the majority of the profits. The self-publisher is in the catbird seat, instead of giving 90 percent to a traditional large publisher. The point again is that success can come through the do-it-yourself method. It's a start, a way to hang in there and maybe beat all the odds against you.

One first novelist in California has made money by selling his self-published novel door-to-door. He has every right to call himself a published author. There's just no telling where a self-publishing venture may lead you. Do your best to find a recognized, traditional publisher for your book – if you choose to go that way. But think about self-publishing if and when you cannot place a book that you have done.

A number of successful writing careers have been launched by self-publishing, and it might just work for you. Once your self-published book proves itself in the marketplace, you will find little trouble placing your next book. Certainly it will be easier than before. An author is only as good as his or her latest book, some say, but a track record can open doors that were previously closed to you.

In short, consider your options with each book you bring to life. Will you go the traditional publisher route, the online publisher, or self-publish it? The choice is yours. And with each new book, you have the same decision to make. Good luck with all your publishing decisions. When you know you published your book *yourself,* and saw it really go places, there will be an extra reward punch there for you. And that can be satisfying as well as profitable.

25
Questions and Answers

❖ ❖ ❖

At one time or another in their lives, many people think that they might have at least one book in them. It's a bit sad that most never even make a start on a book. Who knows? A little encouragement might have helped them to get one written.

Here are some frequently asked questions and answers about writing and selling books. They're meant to offer guidance and encouragement for your own writing.

How much money can I make writing books?

Anywhere from several thousand dollars to millions. Blockbuster books like *The Hunt for Red October, Jaws, The Godfather, Fatherhood, Lake Woebegon Days, The Day After Tomorrow, 2012,* and others have pulled in astronomical amounts. Then again, quite a few books earn from $10,000 to $60,000, up to $80,000 and more for their authors. Well-known authors can earn hundreds of thousands, but a poor to terrible economic era can cut this way down. People continue to buy books, however, even in bad times. Good times or bad, the book will always remain.

Which book publisher has had the most bestsellers over the years?

The last research on this showed that Doubleday was still the leader.

Could a person with just a love for books and reading be a possible future author?

Why not? The potential is certainly there. You will start with a certain feeling, respect, and affection for books. I began this way. I enjoyed reading all kinds of books. I still do. Then one day I just said to myself: "Why don't I write a book after doing all these magazine articles?" I did just that. I'm still at it today and expect to be for the rest of my life. Once book writing gets in your blood, you're hooked.

I would like to write a travel book. What advice can you give me?

Professional writers who specialize in travel books will often take a trip across their native country or some other one. They may take notes and conduct research along the way. After returning home, they write books based on their trips. If done well, travel books can pay off for years or even decades.

When an author sells a first novel or nonfiction book, is it better to stick with that same publisher on future books or play the field?

Many publishers used to include a clause in their contracts giving them an option on the author's next book. This clause is now usually omitted in many contracts. This means authors are not required to send their next books to the publishers of their earlier work. It's optional. An author who has been generally happy with a certain publisher may stick with the same company for years. Other authors remain independent and place their books with a variety of publishers, often signing with the company that offers the best overall deal.

Doesn't it take some inside contacts to sell a book today?

An "inside contact" may give you a better chance to make a sale, but one of the most valuable tools for selling books is persistence.

In the words of Madden Cassidy, a British teacher, "Over the years in my creative writing classes, I've noticed without exception that success comes not to the most talented people but to those, usually a shade less talented, who are really strong on persistence."

What would you say is the most important element needed for writing a bestseller?

Luck, but I think that in the case of a novel, storytelling ability is by far the most important of all. Timing, however, also can have great effect. N. Richard Nash had a novel published at the same time as the cardinals in Rome joined together to choose a new pope. Nash's novel, *The Last Magic*, starts with a pope who is dying. The timing of a book's publication can have an influence on its acceptance and success with the book-buying public.

For a first novel, would I stand a better chance of publication by writing a romance?

Romance novels are still selling though perhaps not as strong as certain earlier periods. Some authorities in the industry say there's a glut of such books on the market, and some publishers of this type of book are not doing as many as they once did. This can change with the passing of time.

The Thorn Birds had a remarkable influence on this type of book, in my opinion. I think it inspired a whole new wave of interest in romance in general. Most agree that women authors have a better feel, or instinct, for writing a romance novel.

How does an author handle the copyright for his or her book?

Copyright laws tend to change fairly quickly, but if you submit your work to a publisher, they will take care of copyright matters for you if they accept your book.

There is really no need for authors to copyright their manuscripts before sending them to publishers. This is because authors are already automatically protected by Common Law Copyright. Then with acceptance of the work, the publisher will secure full copyright. While copyright protection is a large concern for new authors, it is generally not a good idea to secure a copyright before submitting the manuscript. Because publishers are accustomed to taking care of it for authors, receiving an already-copyrighted work can be a bit insulting, as it implies the author thinks the publisher is a thief!

A competent literary agent will handle the various rights to an author's work. Of these various rights, one key question the author (and agent if one is involved) should decide is whether they are offering world rights to a work or only North American rights to the book. The author's literary agent, if he or she has one, will of course handle and negotiate all rights to the book. Most quality literary agents do not offer world rights, preferring to negotiate foreign rights themselves on behalf of the authors they represent.

Don't most authors need a sympathetic editor?

Certainly many do. This is a major reason why many authors prefer to work with an editor who has also done some writing.

Can two or more books be written at the same time?

Some fortunate authors seem to do well with several books in progress at the same time. Keep in mind though, that some of those books are novels, and they have to be able to juggle several series of characters and plots to keep the manuscripts going. That can be tricky. The advantage here is when such authors grow tired of working on one book, or hit a snag with it, they can simply turn to another work in progress.

Other authors cannot turn the writing process off and on so easily for different projects. They prefer to focus on one book at a time. You'll have to experiment to find out the limits of your own powers.

There's an advantage to working on two or three books at the same time if you can manage it. It may help to keep you, the author, from getting stale.

Should an author, whether a newcomer or veteran, write only what he or she knows?

This is an old question that keeps popping up all the time. Many authors would agree with you. Personally, I believe that an author should feel free to write on any subject under the sun that is of interest. Some publishers lose out on good books because they insist that certain subjects be tackled by only experts. Let's face it, most authors would run out of material fast if they had to be experts on each subject they choose. They, in effect, become experts anyway from the research and the interviews they do for many books.

Should an author seek to work with a small, medium or large publisher?

With some success and credits behind you, you should have more clout going for you. You're certainly free to try to sell to publishers of your choice whatever their size may be. Generally speaking, some small publishers may be able to give your book more attention than a large company. The large publishers, however, usually offer the biggest advances, which are important to many authors, and helpful in completing their manuscripts.

Does an author have any control over the retail price of his or her book?

Most publishers (if not all of them) have the last word on a book's price. Some powerhouse, big name authors may express their opinions on the matter of price and thus have an influence in that area.

Must an advance against royalties on a book be paid back by an author if the book does not sell?

Some publishers used to include a clause in their contracts stating that unearned advances had to be paid back. Now an author is usually allowed to keep the advance whatever number of copies the resulting book may sell. There are still some publishers around who may expect the advance back should the book not sell enough copies to cover what was paid the author.

What types of book subjects have the best chance to become bestsellers?

I would say *timeless* subjects that are helpful in some way or another to a large number of readers. This would include self-help books, how-to, general interest, cookbooks, reference, and other categories. The thing to strive for is a book that will continue to be in demand by readers for years to come. To me this means a timeless subject of help to the new readers coming along each year. If the book being written is a novel, then I would say a fascinating read whether that means adventure, science fiction, mystery, detective, western, coming-of-age, romance, historical, thriller, or another genre.

Do you think it's alright to telephone an editor in New York, Chicago, Los Angeles, (or wherever) about a book project?

My answer is a qualified yes. I think it's okay – if you know the editor and have had some correspondence (e-mail or snail mail) with him or her. Otherwise, do *not* phone until you get the editor's okay. A great many editors absolutely hate to be called unless they specifically ask an author to do so or state their okay on it. Some do not mind being called on occasion, providing you know them. First ask if it's okay to call. Most editors are so busy with meetings – and juggling all their books through the process – that they see red when their time evaporates due to author phone calls. Editors are like other people: some are irritated by certain things. Others are not. The bottom line here is get their permission first.

26
Some Parting Advice

❖ ❖ ❖

I believe the following advice will prove to be helpful to you as you write and sell your new books. It's based on my own experience over several decades in the book business. It should and will save you time, effort, and discouragement, but mostly I hope it will inspire you.

Once you find a publisher who treats you fairly and professionally, stick with that company – at least as one publisher you work with on a regular basis – or from time to time as your schedule allows.

Think in terms of what will interest and help your readers.

Every time you offer a manuscript or e-mail a proposal (or snail mail it), realize and accept the fact that you're gambling. Your material may not get there. It may be lost in the mail (it can happen) or even come back to you in somewhat shredded condition. Over a period of years this can happen to about 10 percent of the material you send on its way. Just know that parcels do sometimes go astray in the mails when you use priority mail, which is overall still considered snail mail. Some authors send hard copy manuscripts by priority-insured mail. Others send it slower by regular mail, still using Media Mail. It's a different world today, and more and more authors (if not most today) get their proposals or complete books done first on their computers and can then send the whole thing via e-mail.

Remember always that "the impossible is just something nobody has done yet."

The e-mail query (or snail mail query) gives you psychological insurance. Do not send in material cold to a publisher. If you do, in most cases, your material will end up getting trashed or thrown away. I know there are reports sometimes on how this or that great manuscript "was picked out of a publisher's slush pile" and went on to great success, but it does not happen very often. The first *Harry Potter* manuscript was found in a slush pile, but what I'm telling you is that you can't count on that happening – that incident was one of J.K. Rowling's big breaks. Always e-mail or snail mail a query letter first to see if there is any interest in your project.

Remember that, as an author, you can go anywhere. All you need are pens, pencils, a notebook, paper, a laptop, or place where you have access to a computer. And yes, there are authors around who still use a word processor or typewriter on occasion. Typewriters are practically extinct, though, and considered by most as a relic of the Stone Age. What I want you to remember is authors are some of the freest people in the world. A laptop, a pen, a notebook and you're in business – or at least some phase of it.

Many books are considered successes even though they may sell far less than a 50 thousand or more copy bestseller. Many believe that 40 thousand sold copies is a bestseller.

It's easier to write a book on one subject than to research 20 to 30 different subjects for magazine articles.

Book publishers are in the business of selling ideas.

You should have one or more self-help books in you. This book category will always be with us. Just as one example of many, *How to Win Over Worry* sold 330,000 copies.

Business books can do well in the marketplace and especially if the timing is right for it. My own earlier book, *Money In Your Mailbox: How to Start and Operate A Successful Mail-Order Business* (John Wiley & Sons) went through a number of editions and sold hundreds of thousands of copies and was even translated into foreign editions. I received many letters from readers saying how much the book helped them to make money via mail-order. The book today is considered a classic in its field, which pleases me a lot. All authors want to see their "babies," their books, do well in the marketplace and make a difference in the lives of readers. These are some of the extra benefits of being an author.

If you live outside the New York area, it's usually better to have an agent. This is especially true if the novel is your main interest. Never forget, though, that many authors write *both kinds* of books – nonfiction books *and* fiction. For a change of pace, I even tried my hand at a television script and sold it to Hollywood several years back. My script was produced and shown on the tube to over thirty million viewers. Having this one produced television credit has "opened doors" for me in the film colony, but books remain my main interest. Scripts are a different type of writing, but after doing a number of books I found the change of pace refreshing at the time. I had done an earlier series script at the invitation of Warner Brothers, so I knew something about script writing.

The staple of most book publishers is the trade book. Backlist titles that bring in money year after year do much to keep publishing companies functioning.

Send out many ideas for new book projects. You just cannot tell what might strike an editor's fancy. I personally believe the *timing* for certain book projects can be crucial. A book idea can be hot at one particular time and more or less dead in the water at a different time. Keep this timing factor in mind.

Try to write as if you think writing is fun. It really is hard work for most authors, even if you do sometimes see authors (or would-be authors) batting away on their laptops on airplanes. Many authors think they've had a great day if they get three to five new pages done *per day* – meaning pages they can use.

Many books seek only to entertain the reader and become bestsellers because they do it so well. This goes for both nonfiction books and novels.

In most cases, an outline or synopsis will make it easier to write your book. It gives you a road map. Some authors work as hard (or even harder) on their outlines than the actual manuscripts. Don't spend *all* your energy, all your "ammunition," on the outline and then have nothing left for the manuscript.

The first book an author does is often the hardest. It gets somewhat easier after the first one, but other factors of course come into play. Naturally, some books can be very difficult and painful to write.

"Clear writing is clear thinking." Many a good book has been written on this basic premise.

One good way to stay enthusiastic as an author is to read *Publishers Weekly* from cover to cover each and every week. If you intend to write more than one book, you should subscribe – and I don't get a commission for saying that. Reading *PW* keeps you informed on what's happening in the overall book publishing industry.

It helps to check *Books in Print* (available at your local library) or Amazon.com to see what other books have been published on a particular subject you have in mind, or one that interests you. Know your competition!

Books are noble things. They can bring you possible fame and fortune.

Enough research on a book idea lets you know if your idea is really a good one and worth developing.

Some book outlines don't take too much time. Others require a lot of thought, time, and work, but they can pay off handsomely for you.

One author traveled some sixteen thousand miles all over the nation to visit amusement parks. She was gathering material for a book about *merry-go-rounds*. Unusual ideas like this can and will take you places.

Germany is a big book market. They are big readers in that nation.

Mark Twain convinced Ulysses Grant to write his memoirs for 70 percent of the net profits. The heirs of General Grant realized more than 420,000 dollars in royalties from the two volumes. That was a huge fortune in 1885. It's also very interesting to know that Grant was dying when he was trying to complete his manuscript. This serves as valid *proof* that solid, important books can be written under dire circumstances, great stress, and difficult conditions.

Sherwood Anderson said, "Words are the greatest things ever invented." Remember this well, for words are your stock in trade as an author.

Deadlines in a book contract help an author to finish a project. Most book contracts state when a manuscript is to be delivered. Do your best to meet every deadline. Your editor and publishers will appreciate it.

What makes a book sell, and sometimes take off like a rocket, is usually word-of-mouth recommendation. But anything and everything an author can do for his or her book will help. The internet can sell a lot of the books you write. If you have or develop a website or blog, promote your books. With the web, the world has become your market.

An increasing number of New York publishers tend to go for the big commercial book. They back such books with more money, promotion, and advertising. The fact remains that while some books still sell even if the publisher does next to nothing, you should always do whatever you can to promote each of your books.

Try to get your book (hopefully books) on all the online search engines. By being a crafty author, you can and will increase the odds that your new book will be noticed and bought more often. The more people who know about your books, the more sales you will realize.

Try your hand occasionally at a paperback original – a trade paperback or mass market book. You may be pleasantly pleased with the result.

Remember always that you can write one or more books under a pen name and not your real one.

One book club paid five figures for a book on *knitting*. Try to pick timeless subjects that will be continuous sellers over the years ahead.

If your time and work schedule allow it, attend one writers' conference each year. You will get to meet agents and some of your fellow authors this way. Some of these conferences and seminars for authors are better than others, so find out about them first.

Finally: never give up on a book idea, project, outline, synopsis, or manuscript you still believe in, no matter who rejects it or gives you a thumbs down. The truth is that no big shot agent, publisher, or editor *really knows* where the next blockbuster bestseller is going to materialize. "All things are possible to him [or her!] that believeth." During World War II, when Winston Churchill was visiting a school class – and speaking to the students – he suddenly cracked his cane over an empty school desk and said, in a powerful voice: "Never, never,never, never, never, never give up."

Good luck always with your writing. I hope very much this book will make a difference in your writing career and thus in your life, and that when I reach the "other side," I can see this impact this book has had. It's a great thing to be an author, for you touch the lives of many others. You can have a positive impact on their careers, their work, daily lives, and their future. I wish you all the best with every book you bring into this world. I hope every one of your books will do you proud and impact your readers.

Whatever happens, don't ever stop writing. You're an author. *And don't you forget it.* I'll see you out there – on all those empty pages – waiting for our words.

Index

Advance, 10-11, 150
Agents, 51-58, 63, 140-141, 153-154
And Ladies of the Club, 12
Asimov, Isaac, 12, 14, 61
Auntie Mame, 22

Baker, Samm Sinclair, 131-132
Bestsellers, 16-23, 76-82, 146, 149
    examples, 19, 81-82
    length of, 85-86
    religious books as, 105
    revision of, 89
    writing, 19-23
Benchley, Peter, 9, 16, 125
Blume, Judy, 17-18
Book-of-the-Month Club, 12
Books
    as income, 10-12, 144-145
    first, 6-7, 147, 154
    price, 84-85, 148
    titles, 81-82
Books in Print, 66, 155
Bradbury, Ray, 34

Bradford, Barbara Thomas, 17, 18, 34
Brady, John, 69
Business books, 109-115, 153

Cartland, Barbara, 101
Catton, Bruce, 20
Chapters, 42-47
Chicago Manual of Style, 66
Clancy, Tom, 32, 77, 125
Collaborative writing, 129-132, 156
Coma, 9
The Complete Book of Running, 7
Computer books, 114-115
Cook, Robin, 9
Cookbooks, 8
Copyright, 147-148
The Craft of Interviewing, 69
Cussler, Clive, 16, 19-20, 126-129

The Day of the Jackal, 22
Don't Sweat the Small Stuff, 95, 125

Editors, 57-64, 140-141, 150
    query letters to, 23, 47-49, 152

159

Elements of Style, 66
English the Easy Way, 28
Erskine, John 103
Everything But Money, 28

Fitzgerald, F. Scott, 18-19, 34-35
Fixx, Jim, 7
Freeman, Cynthia, 124

Gardner, Erle Stanley, 12
Ghostwriting, *see* Collaborative writing
Going Rogue, 17
Graham, Billy, 106

Harry Potter (book series), 23, 152
Hemingway, Ernest, 35
How to Write Songs that Sell, 27
How-to books, 91-96
Humor books, 120-123
The Hunt for Red October, 32

In Search of Excellence, 111
Innocent Blood, 7

James, P.D., 7
Jaws, 9, 16
Johnson, Barbara Ferry, 100

The Last Magic, 147
Levenson, Sam, 28
Look Homeward Angel, 89
Lust for Life, 22, 80

Mass-market paperbacks, 124-128

Massie, Robert, 21
Matthews, Patricia, 101
Megatrends, 111
Michener, James, 34, 61
Mitchell, Margaret, 34
Mr. Lincoln's Army, 20

Naisbitt, John, 111
Nash, Richard N., 146
Nicholas and Alexandria, 21
Nonfiction, 24-30
    advantages over fiction, 25
    length, 40, 84-85
    research for, 67
The Nothing Book, 120
Novak, William, 130-131
Novel, 31-36
    length, 40, 83-85
    research for, 67

O'Connor, Donald, 123
The Out-of-Towners (film), 122
Outlines, 37-41, 50

Palin, Sarah, 17
Peale, Norman Vincent, 26
Perkins, Max, 89
Poland, 34
The Power of Positive Thinking, 26
Poynter, Dan, 143
Promotion, 59-60, 133-138, 156
Publisher's Weekly, 51, 78, 155
Publishers, 47-50, 140-141, 146, 149, 151, 156
    and store managers, 119

of humor books, 123
of religious books, 106-107
Puzo, Mario, 126

Raise the Titanic, 16
Reinventing the Corporation, 111
Religious-inspirational, 104-108
Research, 65-69, 71-72
Rinehart, Mary Roberts, 55-56
Robbins, Harold, 6, 125-126
Rogers, Rosemary, 22, 87, 102-103
Romance novels, 97-103, 147
Royalties, 11, 53, 117, 149

Sand, George, 14, 32-33, 74
Santmyer, Helen Hooven, 12-13
Schachter, Norman, 28
Self-publishing, 139-143
Serling, Rod, 20-21
Space, 34

A Stillness at Appomattox, 20
Stone, Irving, 80
Sweet Savage Love, 22, 87

Textbooks, 116-119
Travel books, 145

Wallace, Irving, 90
Wallach, Anne, 6
When Bad Things Happen to Good People, 124
Who's Who, 69
Wolf, Joan, 100-101
Wolfe, Thomas, 89
A Woman of Substance, 17
Words into Type, 66
A World Full of Strangers, 124
Writing, 70-75
help for writer's block, 45
schedule, 73-75

Made in the USA
Charleston, SC
19 October 2012